COMPUTER-AIDED
DESIGN
IN
MANUFACTURING

COMPUTER-AIDED
DESIGN
IN
MANUFACTURING

David Valliere

Prentice Hall, Englewood Cliffs, New Jersey 07632

Library of Congress Cataloging-in-Publication Data

Valliere, David.
    Computer-aided design in manufacturing / David Valliere.
        p.   cm.
    Bibliography: p.
    Includes index.
    ISBN 0-13-165408-X
    1. CAD/CAM systems.   2. Computer-aided design.   I. Title.
    TS155.6.V36   1989
    670'.285--dc20   89-34408
                                                            CIP

Editorial/production supervision and
    interior design: **Brendan M. Stewart**
Manufacturing buyer: **Mary Ann Gloriande**

This book can be made available to businesses
and organizations at a special discount when
ordered in large quantities. For more information
contact:

Prentice-Hall, Inc.
Special Sales and Markets
College Division
Englewood Cliffs, N.J. 07632

 © 1990 by Prentice-Hall, Inc.
A Division of Simon & Schuster
Englewood Cliffs, New Jersey 07632

Printed in the United States of America
10 9 8 7 6 5 4 3 2 1

0-13-165408-X

Prentice-Hall International (UK) Limited, *London*
Prentice-Hall of Australia Pty. Limited, *Sydney*
Prentice-Hall Canada Inc., *Toronto*
Prentice-Hall Hispanoamericana, S.A., *Mexico*
Prentice-Hall of India Private Limited, *New Delhi*
Prentice-Hall of Japan, Inc., *Tokyo*
Simon & Schuster Asia Pte. Ltd., *Singapore*
Editora Prentice-Hall do Brasil. Ltda., *Rio de Janeiro*

For my wife, Nalini

CONTENTS

Preface   xi

Copyrights and Trademarks   xiii

PART ONE   CAD Systems   1

1 **Introduction to Computer
   Graphics and CAD Systems**   3

   1.1   Overview of CAD/CAM
         Systems,   3
   1.2   Hardware Devices,   8

2 **The User Interface to CAD/CAM** 22

2.1 User Input, 22
2.2 File Handling, 28
2.3 File Protection, 30

3 **Two-dimensional CAD Application** 34

3.1 Overview of CADD, 34
3.2 Creation of Entities, 35
3.3 Entity Manipulation, 55
3.4 Other Functions, 61

4 **Three-dimensional CAD Application** 65

4.1 Overview of 3D CAD, 65
4.2 Coordinate Systems, 66
4.3 Views, 67
4.4 Drawings, 69
4.5 Creation of 3D Entities, 70
4.6 Surfaces, 71
4.7 Solids, 74
4.8 Shading, 75

5 **Enhanced Functions of CAD/CAM** 78

5.1 Overview of Enhanced Functions, 78
5.2 Programming, 78
5.3 CAE Analysis, 92

PART TWO   CAD in Computer-integrated Manufacturing   96

6 Computer-integrated Manufacturing Introduction   97

6.1 The Nature of Computer-integrated Manufacturing, 97
6.2 Information Flow and CIM, 98
6.3 Models of CIM, 99
6.4 Developing a CIM Database, 100

7 Computer-aided Manufacturing   106

7.1 Overview of CAM, 106
7.2 Manufacturing Control, 106
7.3 Computer-aided Process Planning, 108

8 Numerical Control Manufacturing   114

8.1 Overview of NC Machining, 114
8.2 CNC Machines, 114
8.3 Programs, 119
8.4 APT Language, 121
8.5 Toolpath Entities in CAD, 122
8.6 Improving CAM, 126

9 Communications   129

9.1 Local Area Networks, 129

9.2   Intersystem Communication
      Translating,   135
9.3   Other Communications,   143

PART THREE   Selection, Implementation,
             and Management of CAD
             Systems   **148**

10 **Selecting and Running the
    CAD System**   **149**

    10.1   System Selection Process,   149
    10.2   Justifying CAD/CAM,   155
    10.3   CAD/CAM Management,   157

11 **Case Study in Selection and
    Implementation**   **161**

    11.1   The Organization,   161
    11.2   Injection Mold Making,   161
    11.3   CAD Application,   163

    **Cross Reference
    of MultipleTerms**   **167**

    References   **169**

    Index   **175**

PREFACE

Computer-aided design (CAD) and other computer-based technologies have the potential to revolutionize the manufacturing workplace. They provide tools by which enormous gains in productivity and efficiency may be realized. However, their effective use is critically dependent on the structure of the organization in which they are used. To fully reap their benefits, major changes in design and manufacturing departments may be required, both in their internal operations and in their dealings with external parties. For managers wishing to implement CAD in their organization in the most effective and productive manner, it is not sufficient simply to select a system and place it before their designers. The key to a productive CAD installation lies in the full understanding of the requirements and capabilities of CAD, and in the willingness of managers to restructure operations to meet those requirements, and to fully utilize those capabilities. It is the goal of this book to provide managers and manufacturing professionals with a sufficiently broad understanding of computer-aided design to effectively implement and run a productive CAD facility.

I began writing this book after working in the field a number of years and realizing that a complete source of information on the effective use of CAD/CAM technology is not currently available. I have seen many companies progressing only through trial-and-error experimentation, with a great many mistakes along the way. Existing books on CAD fall short of providing companies and their managers with the information they need to best use CAD; their emphasis is largely on theoretical discussions of computer graphics. This shortcoming also leaves students of CAD without a source from which to learn the practical operation and management of CAD and its related technologies in the workplace.

The information that I provide in this book has been largely taken from direct observation or from experience gained during years working in CAD/CAM industries. Each of my positions in the industry has brought new insights to the effective operation and management of CAD facilities—insights that I have included throughout this book. From work as a CAD design engineer, I gained firsthand experience with CAD systems from the user's viewpoint—the features of CAD systems that truly made the design work easier, as well as the numerous features that we would have liked to have seen, but were missing from those early CAD systems. Later, I worked as a custom software developer on a large CAD system, developing company-specific enhancement software to tailor the CAD system to particular company needs. The productivity gains that we were able to achieve using this approach highlighted the importance of tailor fitting the CAD system capabilities to the needs and practices of the organization. After a period of software development, I moved into NC programming. Here I discovered the sorry state of automated manufacturing techniques in many Canadian companies, and how the high-level output of the CAD system was being routed through so many archaic processes solely to meet the requirements of NC controller manufacturers who had not kept up with modern computing techniques. A number of plans and suggestions for the improvement of NC manufacturing methods resulted. Later, I assisted a small blow-molding company bring CAD/CAM into their manufacturing operations. This involved strategic cost justifications for the system purchase and development of new operating techniques and procedures for the design and manufacturing departments. Here we successfully employed the new management and operational techniques outlined in this book. Throughout this book, I have drawn on these past experiences, and on the experiences of my colleagues, to provide relevant information that accurately reflects the strengths and weaknesses of using CAD technology.

This book is divided into three parts for ease of reference. Part One deals exclusively with the operation of CAD systems. It provides an overview of the capabilities of CAD systems in drafting, design, and analysis tasks. The discussion is sufficiently general so as to be applicable to CAD systems from a wide variety of vendors. However, where a feature of one particular CAD system is especially noteworthy, it is examined in more detail. This section provides manufacturing professionals with information of sufficient depth to fully appreciate the abilities of CAD technology, while providing students of CAD with an excellent introduction to this application of computer graphics techniques.

Part Two deals with the use of CAD in an overall computer-integrated manufacturing (CIM) environment. It covers the role of CAD in CIM, as well as how CAD operations should be configured to facilitate expansion and the development of a CIM environment. This leads into discussions of the relations between CAD, group technology, process planning, and NC manufacturing. Details of the information-exchange process, between the CAD system and other computer systems, are also given in this section.

Part Three deals with the management of CAD systems. This includes a wide range of topics from the process by which an appropriate CAD system may be selected to the particular management techniques used to operate a CAD facility. It is in this section that the most valuable insights on cost-effective and intelligent operation of CAD systems can be found. Managers of existing or proposed CAD/CAM facilities, and students who aspire to such positions, should make particular note of the information contained in this final section.

I would like to thank several people for their assistance in the development of this book. Special thanks are due Dr. Beno Benhabib (Department of Mechanical Engineering, University of Toronto). Throughout the many revisions of the manuscript, he has been a constant source of insightful criticism and guidance in matters of scope and treatment of the subject. Thanks also to the following people who helped by reading the manuscript and providing many useful comments and suggestions for improvement: Dr. V. Lakshmanan (Ontario Research Foundation), Mr. R. tenGrotenhuis (Cybernetic Perception Systems), Mr. C. Orthlieb (Northern Telecom Canada), Dr. N. K. Mani (State University of New York, Buffalo). Finally, special thanks also to my wife, Nalini, for her support during all the times when I was "off with my computer again."

—David Valliere

COPYRIGHTS AND TRADEMARKS

CADDS4X – Computervision Corp.

ANVIL-4000 – Manufacturing and Design Services Inc.

Unigraphics II – McDonnell Douglas Automation Co.

CATIA – Dassault Systemes

Geomod & Supertab – Structural Dynamics Research Corp.

Design Grafix – Engineering Systems Corp.

Domain – Apollo Computer

Series 7000 – Auto-Trol Technology Ltd.

Empress/32 – Rhodnius Inc.

part one

CAD Systems

This first section of the book deals with computer-aided design systems from the user's viewpoint. It discusses in detail the capabilities of CAD systems and how they may be applied to design tasks.

Chapter 1 starts with an introduction to computer graphics and with an overview of the design applications of computer graphics systems. It also explains the basic hardware components of a CAD system: what they do and how they interact. Chapter 2 covers the user interface to the CAD system, that is, how the user and computer interact and communicate to perform useful tasks. Chapter 3 takes an extensive look at the capabilities offered by a 2D CAD system, from simple entity creation to manipulation of complex drawings. In Chapter 4 the view is expanded to include the additional capabilities available with 3D CAD systems. These additional capabilities are viewed as providing increased functionality, so that a potential user may compare the benefits of using 3D CAD to its increased cost. Finally, Chapter 5 looks at methods of enhancing the function of CAD systems for particular design tasks. This includes the addition of programming capabilities and engineering analysis capabilities.

chapter 1

INTRODUCTION TO COMPUTER GRAPHICS AND CAD SYSTEMS

1.1 OVERVIEW OF CAD/CAM SYSTEMS

Before embarking on a study of the details of CAD/CAM systems and operations, it is important to have an understanding of their full capabilities and some of the diverse uses to which they have been applied. This chapter touches briefly on the overall capabilities of CAD/CAM that are further explored in later chapters. It also looks at the predominant uses of this new technology and its future directions.

1.1.1 Capabilities

What makes the CAD/CAM system such a powerful tool is its many diverse capabilities. It is a synergistic combination of the precision of electronic graphics and the mathematical processing power of the digital computer. This allows the system to serve in a wide variety of uses, from engineering analyses and manufacturing control to the artistic creation of shaded three-dimensional shapes and patterns.

The primary capability that CAD/CAM brings to the user is that of perfect scale drawing. The system allows the user to create accurate scale line drawings in two or three dimensions, to create complex three-dimensional surfaces, and to accurately model complex three-dimensional solids. This is the unique power of CAD/CAM, the capability that sets it apart from other uses of computers.

Next in importance of the capabilities of a full CAD/CAM system is its ability to automatically generate production information based on the geometric model contained in the CAD part. This information can be used in many ways during the manufacturing process. Bills of material can be automatically generated from the CAD parts. Production planning and control information may be used in plant scheduling and management. Automatically calculated and formatted numerical control information may be used in a variety of ways by directing it to different numerically controlled machines or systems. It may be three-axis milling information to direct a milling machine to cut a surface as described in the CAD part, or it may be positional and sequence information to control an entire robotic workcell.

The system also provides the full range of text processing capabilities commonly associated with computers and word processors. Documents can be prepared on the system with a wide range of typefaces or fonts and in a variety of styles. These documents are stored in the computer memory and can be later manipulated in many ways to suit their particular applications.

The abilities to create both graphics and text would be somewhat limited if they were restricted to being separate entities to the system. Most CAD/CAM systems provide methods whereby textual and graphical information can be merged in the creation of more complex documents or drawings. A great deal of flexibility is allowed in how text and graphics may be combined.

The full number-crunching processing power of the digital computer is also exploited by the system in providing the user with a full range of engineering analysis functions and capabilities. The use of finite element methods in component design is an ideal combination of requirements for number crunching and complex graphical displays. This has been provided by CAD/CAM systems with great success.

With the appropriate use of various input devices, the CAD/CAM system can also digitize information about the real world to bring it into the realm of computer processing. Complex coordinate-measuring machines or photodigitizers provide means of capturing geometric information of actual components and supplying it to the CAD/CAM system for analysis or other processing.

The heart of the CAD/CAM system is a digital computer. This computer provides a number of capabilities that are not specific to CAD/CAM but can be developed on any computer. It provides the capability for writing and using a variety of computer programs to be used for calculations or for processing large amounts of information. This information can be of any type, not just that pertaining to the CAD/CAM application of the system.

The communications capabilities of the computer are also used in CAD/CAM. This provides a method for exchanging information with other computers via the established telecommunications networks. This information may be CAD drawing information, CAM machining information, or any other type of information.

1.1.2 Uses

With such a wide variety of capabilities, it is not surprising that the technology offered by CAD/CAM has found many powerful applications. Most rely on only a small subset of the system capabilities, such as mixing two dimensional graphics with text, or simple electronic drafting; few uses have yet been recognized as requiring the full set. It is the flexibility offered by combining various capabilities of the technology for a particular use or application that has lead to its rapidly increasing use. Figure 1.1 illustrates many of these uses

Graphics   The precise drawing capabilities of CAD, combined with 3D modeling and powerful surface shading abilities, have enabled industrial designers and graphic artists to use this technology with success. Proposed parts can be modeled in three dimensions on the system, and viewed and manipulated as real parts. This gives the designer enormous insight into any potential design or esthetic problems with a part design long before any prototypes have been constructed. The graphics capabilities have also been successfully employed in cartographic and geographic applications, and in geotechnical explorations.

Computer-aided Drafting   Precise 2D drawing capabilities and a full range of drafting functions (such as automatic dimensioning of drawings) provide powerful tools for draftsmen in creating technical drawings or engineering plans. Also, the power of the computer in storing and manipulating large amounts of data can be used to replace large drawing vaults and archiving facilities with electronic forms of data storage, such as magnetic tapes.

Computer-aided Design   Designers and engineers can also use the system to provide a flexible design tool. Changes to a design can be rapidly implemented on a CAD system and their effects quickly seen. This allows the designer to try a wide range of "what if" experiments with a design. This freedom translates into improved quality of designs and better productivity of designers.

Computer-aided Engineering   Further along the lines of the "what if" flexibility that the system provides designers is the range of modeling and analysis abilities that the system can provide engineers. Finite element modeling of components under load, flow analysis of fluids in channels, responses of electrical or electronic circuits, static and dynamic analysis of structures and mechanisms, animation of mechanisms, and full simulation of complex systems can all be provided to the engineer by this computer-based technology.

Computer-aided Manufacturing   The connection that CAD/CAM provides between geometric part models and the number crunching power of computers allows it to provide vast productivity improvements in numerical control (NC) programming over manual methods. Part programming can be automatically performed from geometry created during the CAD design stage of product development, while complex 3D geometry that is extremely difficult to manually program can be quickly and easily programmed by the system if the geometric model has been properly defined.

Figure 1.1 Various CAD uses. (Figs A, C–G Courtesy of Integraph Systems Ltd.; B Courtesy of Auto-trol Technology Ltd)

A) Cartographic

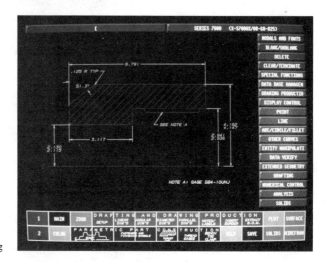

B) Drafting

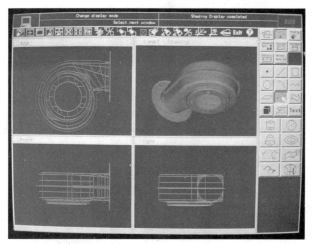

C) Design

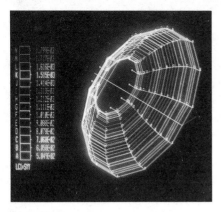

D) Analysis

F) Robotics

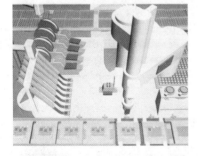

Figure 1.1 (cont.)

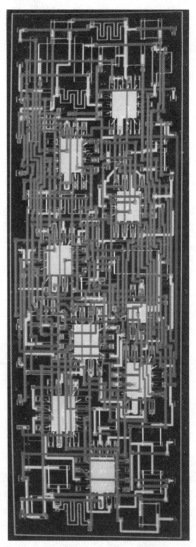

E) Circuit Board Design

G) Engineering

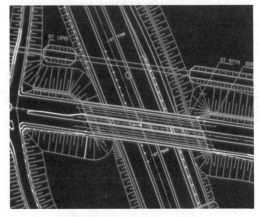

Computer-aided Quality Control   Information on process and quality control can be gathered by a variety of automatic means, from simple passive sensors to complex coordinate-measuring machines. This information can then be fed back into the system and compared to design specification or model tolerances. In this way, the information contained by the system can be used to improve the quality control procedures available to a manufacturer.

Robot Programming   Another use of the system is in offline robot programming. This is made possible because the robot and its working environment can be accurately modeled in the CAD system. This model is then used to develop and test operating programs for the robot. The programmer can then see potential difficulties with a program and resolve them without adversely affecting the downtime of a robot that is in production use.

1.2   HARDWARE DEVICES

The most visible part of the CAD/CAM system is the computer hardware that it runs on. Included in this are CAD workstations, computer terminals, and the computer itself. This section looks at the primary components of the CAD/CAM system: output devices, input devices, storage devices, and processors

1.2.1   Screen Devices

The screen devices present the current state of a CAD part in visual form. It is from the screen that the user may digitize locations on a drawing to construct entities, or may pick existing entities for modification. The screen is most often based on CRT technology, although other methods of dynamic display are possible.

There are two families of screen devices: the refresh screens and the storage screens. Refresh screens do not store any information about the graphics they are displaying, and so must be continually redrawn or refreshed. The information about the graphics to be displayed is stored by the computer in a refresh buffer, the contents of which are continually retransmitted to the screen device. The rate at which this refreshing occurs depends on how long it takes for a single screen refresh to fade from the screen. Unless the refreshes occur faster than this, an annoying flicker of the screen graphics will be apparent.

The most common of the refresh screens is the standard CRT screen. This operates by directing a beam of electrons, produced at the rear of the tube, against a phosphor layer on the face of the tube. The phosphor which is struck by the beam glows for a short period (0.1 to 0.5 seconds). The beam is directed by variably charged plates located in the middle of the tube. As electrons are attracted to positive charges, these plates can be used to deflect the beam and cause it to strike any particular point on the phosphor screen. Figure 1.2 shows the layout of the components in a CRT.

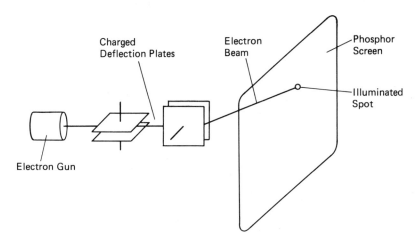

Figure 1.2   CRT component layout

Another recently developed refresh screen is the gas plasma screen, which operates on an entirely different principle than the CRT screen. It consists of three layers forming a flat rectangular sheet. The first layer is a series of closely-spaced fine wires running horizontally. The last layer is a similar series of wires running vertically. Between these two layers lies a layer of gas, such as neon, that fluoresces when ionized. By applying a positive voltage to a horizontal wire and a negative voltage to a vertical wire, a small region of gas can be made to ionize and glow. This appears as a bright dot at the intersection of the two wires. When the voltage is removed from the wires, the gas quickly returns to its normal state, so this screen must be continually refreshed like the CRT screen. The plasma screen is illustrated in Figure 1.3.

Storage screens, in contrast, do not require constant refreshing. Patterns drawn on them remain until they are specifically removed. The storage version of the CRT screen differs only slightly from the standard CRT. In this, a nonconducting charge-storage layer is placed between the electron beam and the phosphor layer. The electron beam strikes the charge-storage layer, charging it, and then the phosphor screen, illuminating a dot. When the beam moves on, the charge is maintained in the charge-storage layer. Also, a low-power flood beam is added to the CRT after the deflection plates. The flood beam evenly illuminates all of the charge-storage layer. Although alone it is not powerful enough to illuminate the phosphor, the flood beam can combine with the stored charge to illuminate those areas of the screen where the main electron beam has been. Figure 1.4 illustrates this device.

The majority of CRT screens, as well as all plasma screens, operate in a rasterizing mode. In this mode of operation, the graphics to be displayed are divided into many horizontal lines called rasters. In the case of the CRT, the electron beam is swept along each of these horizontal raster lines in turn. Wherever a raster line

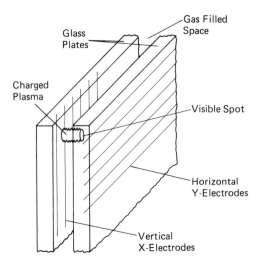

Figure 1.3   Plasma screen layout

intersects a graphical entity to be displayed, the electron beam is turned on and causes a spot to appear on the screen at that location. This process is followed for every raster line on the screen. The collection of all the spots thus illuminated on the screen then appears as the display of the solid graphical entity, provided of course that the rasters are spaced sufficiently close to allow the individual spots to appear to merge into a continuous line.

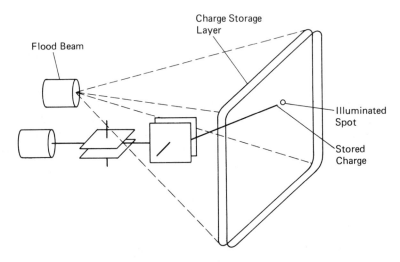

Figure 1.4   Storage screen layout

Some CRT screens, especially storage screens, operate in a vector mode. In this mode of operation, the electron beam is swept in a continuous fashion and in a controlled direction so as to draw an individual entity on the screen. It is then switched off and directed to where the next entity should begin. It then draws the next entity using the same method.

Rasterized graphics lack the crisp appearance of vector graphics. This is partly due to the aliasing effects that occur when the true position of the entity does not lie evenly on spots on successive raster lines. This is most predominant with lines that are at a 45-degree angle to the raster lines. These lines also have the shortcoming that, since their individual raster spots are widely spaced, their brightness is reduced relative to other lines. Figure 1.5 shows how these problems arise with rasterized graphics. Rasterizing also has the drawback of requiring a processor to convert the graphics information into individual on/off spot information to control the electron beam during its pass along each raster.

In spite of these problems, raster screens remain more popular than vector screens. Three factors may account for this. First, the beam control in a vector screen needs to be more versatile and precise, making them more expensive. Second, the rasterizing software required to convert graphics to raster information is well developed and inexpensive. Finally, there is a difference which is crucial for many applications. Simply stated, vector screens cannot shade or fill in closed polygons. This arises from the strictly linear drawing method that vector screens employ. However, raster screens need only illuminate all spots on a raster that lie between the polygon boundaries to achieve filling of the polygon or area. So, any system that is to employ shading or polygon filling in its graphical output must use raster screens.

1.2.2 Input Devices

A wide variety of devices enables a user to input information to the CAD/CAM system. This is due to the ongoing experimentation and development with devices that facilitate the user's input of the four different types of information

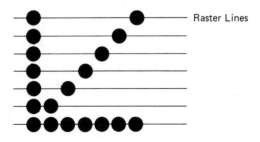

Figure 1.5   Effect of line angle on intensity.

that can be supplied to the CAD/CAM system. These are (1) *entity picking* (where the user indicates one or more existing CAD entities on the screen by pointing to them with a graphics cursor and then alerting the system), (2) *position locating* (where the user indicates a position in the CAD part by moving the graphics cursor there and alerting the system), (3) *text entry* (which is usually achieved via a keyboard) and (4) *valuation* (where the user supplies a value for a system parameter by modifying the position of a dial or switch, either physically or by virtual devices displayed on the screen). Some input devices are illustrated in Figure 1.6.

KEYBOARD

- The keyboard is the most useful and versatile device for performing all of the nongraphical functions of the system. It can be used to enter commands directly to the system or to choose commands from a menu displayed on the screen.
- The most common layout is the ANSI X4.22-1983, or QWERTY layout. Other layouts have been experimented with, such as alphabetical or Dvorak, but have not been found to be conclusively better for most typists.
- Programmable function keys are a useful feature to have on a keyboard. They can be programmed by the user to output long or complex commands at the touch of a single key.
- A separate numeric keypad is an essential feature of a CAD workstation keyboard, since many of the data entered are in numeric form. A separate numeric pad can speed this considerably.
- Edit keys, such as delete, backspace, and insert should also be available to facilitate the user in entering text information.
- Certain keys that can cause damage to the part, or confusion to the user if accidentally pressed at the wrong time, should be protected. This may involve physically protecting the keys by locating them separately from the main keyboard, or covering them with hinged covers, or by requiring the user to press a combination of keys that could not be accidentally pressed, before the potentially dangerous function is executed. For example, the simultaneous pressing of three keys might be required before initiating a complete reset of the workstation.

FUNCTION KEY

- Some systems provide a separate keyboard of nonprogrammable functions keys. These keys are used to invoke commands, call particular menus to the screen, or make selections from a menu.
- It is important in designing the use of such a keyboard to always place similar operations or subfunctions under the same function key; if every menu has an option for returning to the previous menu, that option should be located under the same function key on every menu. This allows the user to develop a muscle

A) Function Keys

B) Tablet

C) Mouse

D) Lightpen

E) Valuator

Figure 1.6 Input devices.

memory of where certain operations are located. This greatly speeds the use of the CAD/CAM system.

TABLET

- The tablet allows the user to control the position of the graphics cursor by direct movement of the hand. It consists of a large planar tablet surface and a puck or pen that is moved over it. The tablet contains an embedded matrix of fine wires that can sense an electric field produced by the puck and thereby provide the system with the puck position. The graphic cursor is then updated to that position.
- The puck usually contains push buttons that are used to alert the system to pick an entity or to digitize a position.

MOUSE

- The mouse is very similar to a tablet with a puck. The only difference is that the tablet itself has been dispensed with. The mouse can internally sense its own motion, either optically or by the mechanical rotation of wheels or a ball, and send this information to the system to update the cursor position.
- The mouse is operated by moving it along the top of a desk or table. The absence of a large tablet makes the mouse a better choice for workstations where space may be limited.
- The mouse also contains alerting buttons for use in entity picking or location digitizing.

JOYSTICK

- The joystick allows the user to move the graphics cursor by simply adjusting the angle of a lever. An alerting button is placed on the top of the joystick to allow location digitizing and entity picking.
- Position joysticks map their displacement angle to a particular location of the cursor on the screen. If the user wants the cursor to be at the left side of the screen, he or she angles the joystick to the left and leaves it there.
- Velocity joysticks map their angle to a direction and speed of cursor movement. Larger angles of the joystick result in faster movements of the cursor, while the joystick must be in its center position to keep the cursor stationary.
- Velocity joysticks require a high speed-to-angle mapping to allow the user to rapidly move the cursor about the screen. However, they also require a low speed-to-angle mapping to allow the user to accurately place the cursor at a particular location. They also require a certain dead band near the center of their range so that the user can stop the cursor without having to place the joystick in its exact center position. These three requirements can be met by a nonlinear mapping function such as in Figure 1.7.

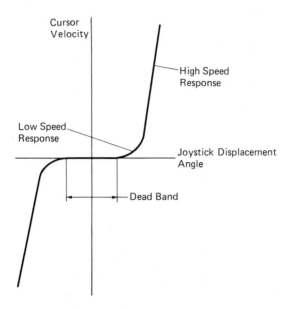

Figure 1.7   Joystick mapping function

LIGHTPEN

- The lightpen is used to point directly at positions or entities on the screen. It contains a photosensor in its tip that senses the light emitted by points on the screen. It often has buttons on its side, or built into the tip, that alert the system. Entities are picked by pointing the lightpen at them on the screen and alerting the system. The system determines which entity is desired by noting when, during the raster scan of drawing the screen, the pen first senses light. That point will be from the drawing of the entity desired. Position digitizing is similarly done. The user points the pen at the screen location and alerts the system. This system responds by sequentially illuminating each point on the screen. When the pen first senses light, the position has been determined.
- Some lightpens are used to control the position of a graphics cursor; the cursor tracks the movement of the pen across the screen. This tracking is accomplished by having the cursor drawn as four lines meeting at a common point. As each line is drawn, the point at which it is first seen by the pen is noted. From these four points the new position of the pen can be calculated (see Figure 1.8). The cursor is then redrawn at that new position. If the pen is moved too rapidly across the screen, tracking may be lost. If this happens, the system initiates a relocating algorithm. In this, points on the screen are successively illuminated in a spiral fashion starting from the last known position of the pen. This ever-widening spiral will eventually be sensed by the pen, thereby reestablishing its location.

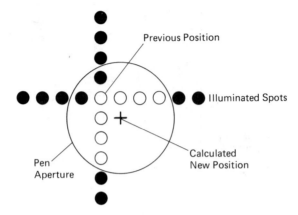

Figure 1.8   Lightpen cursor tracking.

VALUATOR

- Valuators provide a method of changing the value of continuously variable system parameters. Rotary dials are the most common form of the device, but levers or slide controls are also seen. Typically, valuators control the zoom in or out of a part, pan from left to right or up and down, and rotations of the part.
- The valuator may also be provided as a virtual device. In this case, a symbol is displayed on the screen to represent a valuator device and its current setting. The user can then change the setting value by using the graphics cursor control provided by another input device. In this way, the operation of a valuator has been provided without requiring an actual physical valuator device.

TRACKBALL

- The trackball provides the same control over the graphics cursor as a position joystick. The rotational motion of the ball is mapped to a movement of the cursor on the screen. When the ball is stationary, so is the cursor.
- These are rugged devices and have been widely used by the military. They suffer one drawback however; they do not have integral push buttons to alert the system to digitize or pick. Therefore, the user must move his or her hand from the ball to the button in order to perform a pick operation, or use both hands to perform a pick.

TOUCH SCREEN

- This device enables the user to pick entities on the screen by simply pointing to them. It consists of a sensitive layer that is placed on the face of the screen. When the user presses against the layer, the system is alerted and the location pressed is determined. This pointing by finger is the most natural of user interfaces, however, it does not give very fine resolution. For this reason, the touch screen is usually not suitable where digitizing locations requires much accuracy.

VOICE

• Recently, voice-sensitive input devices have been developed. These consist of a microphone and memory where voice patterns are stored. The user must first teach the device the sound patterns for a number of key words that will be used to control the system. The user then is able to operate the CAD/CAM system simply by speaking into the microphone. If the system is unsure about a particular word spoken, it will prompt the user for confirmation. Current systems have vocabularies in the hundreds of words, although research systems have been developed with 20,000-word vocabularies.

SONIC PEN

• This was an early developed device that seems to have dropped in popularity, although it is currently one of very few devices capable of digitizing locations in three dimensions. It consists of a pen with a sound-producing element, such as a spark gap, at its tip. Strip microphones are then arranged perpendicular to the axes. When the user wishes to digitize a location, he or she presses a button on the pen, which causes a sound to be emitted. The time that elapses between the sound creation and its subsequent detection by a strip microphone is proportional to the distance of the pen from the microphone. Thus, the three-dimensional pen location may be computed.

POLHEMUS SENSOR

• This is a recently developed device used to track the position and orientation of an object, such as a pointer, in three-dimensional space. It is a more sophisticated implementation of the approach pioneered by the sonic pen. It consists of an electromagnetic transmitter mounted on the object, containing three transmitter antennae, and three stationary receivers, each containing three receiving antennae. The transmitting and receiving antennae are mounted at right angles to one another, thereby defining a Cartesian coordinate system. The transmitter sends a series of pulsed radiation which induces currents in the receiver antennae. These currents depend on both the distance from transmitter to receiver and their relative orientations. From the nine induced currents, the sensor can deduce the position and orientation of the transmitter relative to the receivers. At the time of writing, this sensor had just been released by the Polhemus Navigation Sciences division of McDonnell Douglas Corporation and had not been applied to any CAD/CAM systems. However, its obvious application as a 3D position digitizer makes it a prime candidate for use in this field [Foley 1987].

DATAGLOVE

- This is another of the advanced input devices that has a promising future in CAD/CAM applications, although it has not yet left the research stage. It has been in development since 1984 at VPL Research Inc. in California. It consists of a glove with numerous fiber-optic cables embedded in it. LEDs at the wrist send light down the fibers, to be received by phototransistors at the other end. Where the cables pass finger joints, they have been treated so that any bending of the cable will cause a fraction of the carried light to leak out. These losses are then detected by the phototransistors. The cables are arranged in the glove so as to detect all abduction and flexion angles of the finger joints [Foley 1987].

- The output from the DataGlove are data that fully describe the arrangement of the user's hand. With appropriate CAD system software, this input device could enable a user to virtually grasp and manipulate the CAD model on the screen. Entities could be transformed and edited by the touch of the user's hand, while viewing rotations could be easily and naturally performed.

1.2.3 Storage Devices

The input devices previously listed provide many methods of getting information into the system, but once there it must be stored. This storage must be in an offline manner, or the memory capacity of the computer will quickly be exhausted. However, if the information is to be often used and accessed, the storage method must also provide for fast retrieval of the information into the computer's main memory. Hard disks are most often used for this purpose. Each disk can store an enormous amount of data, from 20–30 Mbytes/disk on small systems to 300 Mbytes/disk or more on larger systems, while still providing rapid access and retrieval of the data. A typical hard-disk device for a mainframe computer consists of a number of rotating disks of magnetic recording material. These are read from and written to by magnetic read/write heads that move over the disk surfaces in much the same way as a phonograph arm. In a CAD/CAM system, hard disks are most often used to store parts or programs that are currently being worked on or otherwise used. Other CAD parts and programs, which belong to completed jobs, are moved onto one of the less expensive but slower accessed storage media.

Large mainframe systems typically use magnetic tape for this longer term storage purpose. This tape is available on different sizes of reels, the largest of which is capable of holding close to 100 M bits of data. Compared to disk storage, tape storage is very inexpensive; however, it does suffer from slow retrieval speeds. This is primarily due to the sequential access nature of tapes being much slower than the random access of disks. The entire previous contents of the tape must be read before reading can begin on the desired data. Once this reading begins, it also occurs at a slower rate than reading from a hard disk, as the data transferral rate to and from tape is slower than that for disks.

On smaller systems, or systems made up of networks of interconnected small processors, data are often stored on floppy disks. Floppy disks are small removable disks that can store correspondingly smaller amounts of data. Low-capacity disks might store only 360 kbytes of data, while higher-capacity floppy disks can store up to several Mbytes of data. The removable nature of floppy disks makes them a desirable storage medium for sites where several separate small CAD/CAM systems may be required to share information. The floppy disks can simply be moved from one system to another, although this method is hardly taking advantage of modern communications technology. Much better would be to define a communications link between the relevant systems. A continuing use of floppies is in the storage of boot programs for many computers, including most CAD/CAM computers, because of the relative simplicity of controlling floppy disk drives from low firmware levels.

Finally, another available tape-based storage medium is datacassettes. These are small cassettes of magnetic tape, capable of fast reads and writes, although they are still limited by the sequential access nature of all tapes. Datacassettes are commonly used for backups, meaning that they are used to store emergency replacement copies of all parts or files that have been modified on the system since the creation of the last backup cassette. The actual procedures used in creating backups will be discussed in more complete detail in Chapter 10 of this book.

1.2.4 Hardcopy Devices

Hardcopy devices allow the user to transcribe information from the screen of the computer terminal to permanent physical form. This information may be either textual or graphical, so a variety of devices and hardcopying methods have been developed. Broadly, these devices fall into two categories: printers (which are primarily text-handling devices), and plotters (which are primarily graphics handlers). These are not firm and absolute distinctions, as there are some graphical forms that can be handled by printers and most plotters can also handle text.

Four streams of printer technology have been developed. These are, in order of increasing print quality, sophistication, and expense: dot matrix, daisy wheel, ink jet, and laser. Of these, only laser printers have the capability of printing graphics of sufficient resolution for use in CAD drawings. This technology is the combination of xerography and ultra fine raster scanning. Essentially, the page image is computed and broken into individual horizontal scan lines of alternating light and dark regions. A laser then copies these scan lines onto a selenium drum, ionizing it wherever the dark regions occur. The ionized drum areas electrostatically attract particles of black toner, which then form the page image on the drum. This image is then transferred by heat onto a sheet of paper or other hard copy media.

Since the laser printer works from a computer generated page image and not from predetermined character-creation methods such as dot matrices or types, it is capable of reproducing any image onto a page. This allows the laser printer to print any combination of text and graphics onto the same page, at a resolution that is limited only by the width of the laser beam itself.

Similar to the laser printer, but used for creating much larger drawings, is the electrostatic plotter. Drawings are produced from rolls of paper up to 42 inches wide. A writing head is placed horizontally across the paper to create a single raster scan line in one write operation. It directly ionizes the paper at a typical resolution of 200 dots per inch. The paper is then passed through a toner bath, where toner particles adhere to the ionized part of the paper. The paper then leaves the plotter and is cut to length by the user.

Another form of plotter is the pen plotter, or vector plotter. It does not work by rasterizing an image of the drawing to be produced. Rather, it draws lines and arcs directly on the page in continuous motions of a pen. Text is created by writing individual characters. This type of plotting requires that the plotter be able to work on the entire range of the sheet of paper at once. This can be accomplished in two ways. First, the sheet can be placed on a horizontal bed that the pen is free to move over. Otherwise, the paper can be draped over a drum. The plotter may then rotate the drum to bring distant areas of the paper under the pen.

1.2.5 Processors

The heart of the CAD/CAM system and the single most important piece of hardware in it is clearly the computer processor that drives it. From a user's or manager's viewpoint, there is little variation in processors; there are only three fundamentally different processor technologies to be considered. They are clearly separable on criteria of computing speed and power, number of users supported, and future expandability.

The simplest CAD/CAM technology is driven by microcomputers. These offer low-cost CAD/CAM at the expense of all three processor criteria. They are somewhat limited in their processing power (although rapid increases are being made), they typically support only one user, and they have few ways in which they can be expanded to handle increased future demands short of buying more PC-based CAD/CAM systems. These systems have seen some limited success in computer-aided drafting and in production of simple technical drawings, although their limited power has kept them from serving in the highly computation-intensive areas of complex 3D CAD, engineering analysis, and computer-aided manufacturing. This restriction is a result of vendor recognition of the limitations of microcomputer processing power. They have offered only subsets of full CAD/CAM capabilities in order to make their software execute on the microcomputer without unreasonable overheads or lengthy response times. Because the CAD facilities available on microcomputers are so limited at present, they will not be considered further in this book. This book focuses on the full rich set of functions available with minicomputer and mainframe CAD systems.

The full realization of the potential of CAD/CAM requires the processing power of a minicomputer or a mainframe computer. These systems offer full CAD/CAM capabilities to many users; minicomputers can support five to ten users typically, while mainframes can handle many more. Often the multitasking and multiuser capabilities of the processor are not the limiting factor in determining the number of users that may make simultaneous use of the CAD system; it is the response speed of the processor. As the number of users accessing the processor increases, the response time of the processor to an individual request also increases. Because of the methods used by the processor to manage multiple users, the response time can increase rapidly as more users are added. The relationship becomes highly nonlinear. It is the requirement of the response time being better than an arbitrary value that sets the practical limit on the number of users of the CAD system. One common rule of thumb is a limit of no more than two seconds response time for simple tasks, such as deleting a line [Foley & VanDam 1982].

The newest development in processors of CAD/CAM has been in local area networks (LANs). These networks consist of many processors and workstations linked together, allowing all users to share all resources of the network. Processing power can be provided to a user on a demand basis; highly computation-intensive tasks draw on the power of several network processors, releasing them when no longer required. This technology is covered more completely in Chapter 9.

PROBLEMS

1.1 A workstation has a high-resolution CRT display which can display 1,024 × 1,024 unique pixels. Each pixel needs 6 bits of information to display, 3 colors (red/green/blue) × 2 bits of intensity information for each color gun. The screen refresh rate is 30 Hz. What data transfer rate (bit/s) is required from the processor to the screen?

1.2 A particular vector display screen can draw 10,000 vectors per second. The CAD software running on the workstation displays circles as 100-sided polygons. If a user draws a part consisting of a rectangular plate with 500 holes, how long will it take to draw this part on the screen?

1.3 One variation of the function keyboard is a chord keyboard. It consists of five function keys which can be pressed in combinations. Up to five keys can be simultaneously pressed to select a particular function.

   a. How many individual function keys would be needed to replace such a chord keyboard?

   b. If we allow up to three successive function keys pressed in sequence to select a particular function, then how many function keys can the chord keyboard replace?

1.4 What are the relative merits and disadvantages of position and velocity joysticks? Which do you think would be easier to use?

1.5 Lightpens have a potential problem arising from parallax effects. Assume a case where the tip is 3 mm diameter, the glass on the face of the CRT is 1/8 inch thick, and the user is viewing a position digitize from an angle of 15 degrees from vertical. What is the maximum error in position selection that can arise due to parallax?

chapter 2

THE USER INTERFACE
TO CAD/CAM

2.1 USER INPUT

To users, the most important feature of a CAD/CAM system is how it appears to them. The design of the data input interface and the methods by which users may control it are critical factors to the overall productivity of the system. The four aspects of input that must be considered for CAD/CAM are: the command entry method, the screen position locating method, the entity picking or identifying method, and the viewing control method. Each of these factors will be considered in turn.

2.1.1 Menus and Commands

Command input is the heart of the user input interface. It defines how the user will instruct the system as to which function to perform. Various methods of providing this interface have been developed and offered by vendors. Some of these have provided great flexibility to the user and have followed the results of ergonomic research. Some, unfortunately, have not.

Input interfaces have been developed along the two different lines of menus and commands. Menus group all of the system functions into a hierarchy of functions, subfunctions, and subsubfunctions. These are then presented to the user in a series of menus or panels. The user makes a selection from the displayed menu by pressing a key on the keyboard or on a function keyboard. The system then responds by displaying another related menu, or by performing a particular function. Menu-based systems have two advantages over command-based systems. The first is that the system is easy to learn, as all relevant options to a particular operation are displayed on the menu for consideration; no memorizing is required. The second is the muscle memory that is developed in repetitive selection of common functions via a function keyboard. Proficient users do not actually need to read the menus and make the selections to achieve the desired function. They develop muscle memory skill, similar to that of musicians, to unconsciously control their fingers to automatically make all the correct selections to reach the desired function.

Two types of menu-based input interfaces are available:

FIXED MENU

- As its name implies, this type of menu has the arrangement of functions and subfunctions permanently set in the menu system. This can be inconvenient if a particular function often used by the user requires a great number of selections to be made in order to reach the desired menu. Some examples of CAD systems using this approach are the McAuto Unigraphics system and the Dassault Systems CATIA system.

FLEXIBLE MENU

- This type of menu system allows the user to redefine the placement of selection options on the various menus. This makes it possible to place frequently used commands at higher positions in the hierarchy, thereby reducing the number of function keystrokes required.

The second line of input interface development has resulted in command-based systems. These systems require the user to enter command sequences from the keyboard to control the operation of the system. New users often find this type of system difficult to learn because it requires the user to memorize all of the commands and options available at any point in the construction of a drawing. However, more experienced users often prefer it because it allows them to input any command at any time, without having to step through several menus of undesired commands and options.

Two types of command-based input interfaces are also available:

DIRECT COMMANDS

- Direct entry of commands offers the ultimate in flexibility to the user. Any command, with any option, may be typed in when desired. No time is spent in rejecting proffered alternatives from a menu. However, of all input interfaces, this places the most severe demands on the user's memory.

```
# INSert LINe HORizontal:

   key-in from keyboard
         CADDS4X
```

```
POINT              PT-PT              0.0
LINE               PARALLEL
ARC                NORMAL
  .                BISECT
  .                ANGLE
  .                COMPON
                   TANGENT
                   MEAN

select from        select from        key-in from
32 key             screen menu        keyboard
function
keyboard
                   CATIA
```

Figure 2.1   Command input vs. menus.

COMMAND TABLETS

- This is a combination of command entry and menu selection in order to reduce the memory requirement of the user, and to reduce the amount of typing required. In this system, the commands are arranged on a tablet with their options. The user selects the desired commands from the tablet. This has the effect of sending the equivalent string of typed characters to the computer. It is very much like having a menu system where all menus are displayed simultaneously, allowing random access to all the commands. The Computervision CADDS 4X system is a typical example.

Figure 2.1 shows typical examples of direct command input and fixed menu input. Both input methods create horizontal lines.

2.1.2 Position Locating

The second major aspect of the input interface to the CAD/CAM system is its position-locating or digitizing method. The goal of this is to provide the user with a simple method of precisely specifying positions in the CAD part file to serve as data for a command. This positional data may indicate where to place an entity, or supply data for the creation parameters of an entity. Simple screen digitizing is done by positioning a graphics cursor or crosshair at the desired location in the drawing, using one of the input devices mentioned previously, and pressing an alerting or digitizing button. The system then calculates the coordinates of the cursor position and supplies this information to the currently executing command.

Positions can also be defined by the entry of coordinate values. In this arrangement, the user simply types in the values of the various position coordinates. The coordinates may be measured in a number of different, user-selectable coordinate systems.

There are also a number of methods by which position digitizing can be restricted to allow greater control, and thereby be combined with the coordinate-entry method. These have the effect of altering the location data derived from the graphics cursor position to meet other user-defined criteria.

The simplest of these criteria is in requiring particular coordinate values for one or more axes. The user may command the system to take the y-coordinate from the position of the cursor, but force the x-coordinate to be 10.0, for instance. This provides a method of combining the two position-locating methods.

An extension of the concept of forcing coordinates to particular values is the use of grids. Grids serve to define an array of locations of constant x and y spacing that are allowable digitizable screen locations. These grid positions are controlled by user definable spacings and rotation angle from horizontal. Any digitizing of the screen is adjusted to fall onto one of the grid locations. This can be very useful in freehand sketching, as the user can set the grid spacing to be integral multiples of the dimension unit size and freehand sketch parts of clean integral dimensions—roughly horizontal lines will be adjusted to be precisely horizontal, vertical lines will be vertical.

Position locating can also be controlled to fall onto existing entities. This is extremely useful in creating entities that must match each other at particular locations, such as lines meeting at a common point. Six digitizing modifiers are available to force location data into desired relations with existing entities:

1. *End*   This modifier adjusts the digitized position to the nearest endpoint of an entity. A search is made from the true digitized position for the closest entities. The endpoints of these entities are then calculated, and the nearest one used as the selected position.

2. *Int*   This modifier returns the coordinates of a point of intersection between two entities. The user picks the two entities near the desired point of intersection (in the case where there are multiple intersections), and the system calculates the coordinates of their common intersection point.

3. *Near*   This modifier returns the coordinates of the point on the nearest entity that is nearest to the true digitized position.

4. *Orig*   This returns the coordinates of an origin point of a user-selected entity. The nature of an origin point varies with the entity type. The origin of a line is its midpoint, a circle its center.

5. *Pos*   This modifier requires the user to enter a parameter value from 0 to 1. The returned location will be the position on a selected entity that is the specified proportion along its arc length. In the case of a line entity, a Pos 0.5 results in the midpoint of the line.

6. *Angl*   This modifier alters a location to be on the circumference of a selected circle, at a specified angle from horizontal.

Digitized positions can further be modified by applying offsets to the coordinates. Although the coordinate values are usually expressed in rectangular coordinates, these offsets can be specified in many different coordinate systems: Cartesian, polar, cylindrical (3D), and spherical (3D). To use this method of position locating, the user would first digitize a position using any of the other methods. He or she would next input values for the coordinate offsets. The system would then apply the offsets; modified values of the coordinates would then be supplied to the executing command.

Finally, there is a method whereby the user can enter a continuous stream of data points that reflect the path that the user sweeps the graphics cursor through. This stream digitizing works by rapidly sampling the cursor position (say at ten times per second) as the user sweeps it. Each of these sampled locations is then supplied as a separate position. Options are also available to help reduce the amount of data required to specify a given curve with sufficient accuracy by eliminating redundant point data. Two separate criteria can be applied to choose which data points may be discarded. The first is an angular criterion. In this test, a point N is only accepted if a line drawn from point $N+1$ to point N and a line drawn from point $N-1$ to point N intersect with a minor angle that is greater than a user-defined limiting angle. This causes the system to reject points that are essentially collinear, as they supply little information in defining the shape of the overall curve. The second criterion is based on distance. In this test, a point N is only accepted if the distance from point $N-1$ to point N is greater than a user-defined minimum distance. This causes the system to reject points that are so closely spaced as to define impractically short segments of the curve. Both of these criteria then aid in reducing the number of streamed points that are necessary to store in order to define a swept curve.

2.1.3 Entity Picking

Many CAD/CAM system commands require the user to identify or pick the entities that are to be considered or effected by the system. This is done by moving the graphics cursor close to the desired entity and pressing a particular picking button. Since it is difficult for the user to place the cursor directly on the desired entity, so as to unambiguously specify the choice, the system considers each entity to be surrounded by a virtual gravity-field region. Any entity pick that occurs with the cursor inside the gravity field of a particular entity is treated as a pick of that entity. This allows the user to be less precise in pick locations yet still obtain predictable results. This function is closely related to the near modifier of position digitizing, where digitizes in the region surrounding an entity are converted to digitizes on the entity itself.

A further increase in this flexibility is achieved by broadening the effective area of the cursor itself. An area called a *trap region* can be defined around the graphics cursor. With the trap region in effect, any digitizes of the cursor position are translated into potential digitizes of all points in the trap region. Therefore, if any of the cursor trap region overlaps any part of an entity gravity-field region, that entity will be successfully picked.

The user can restrict the selection of entities in picking by setting include and exclude masks. These masks list sets of entity types that may or may not be accepted by the system as results of an entity pick. The masks may be set to allow only the selection of lines, or to allow any entity type except points, or any other combination.

Large groups of entities that lie in one area on the screen may be picked simultaneously by the use of window picks. Windows provide a method of enclosing areas of the screen and processing entities depending on their relation to the window boundary, that is, whether they are inside, outside, or crossing the window boundary. Simple rectangular windows may be defined by digitizing two diagonally separated locations on the screen. Polygonal windows may be specified by successively digitizing all of the vertices of the polygon until closure of the window is obtained. Screen windows can also be used where all entities currently displayed on the screen are treated together by the system. A typical application of this pick method is to quickly delete a large number of entities in a particular region of the part.

Entities can also be gathered into collective structures called *groups*. Groups allow the user to pick several associated entities with a single pick operation. The grouped entities can even be widely separated in a case where windows would not be feasible. The pick of a group always results in the pick of all of the associated entities regardless of their position. On most systems, groups can also be collected into other groups so that a hierarchical structure of groups is formed. Such systems must also provide a means of controlling the level in the hierarchy at which the selection will take place, that is, which set of grouped entities will be included in the pick.

Entities can also be gathered during picking by the use of a chaining modifier. With the chaining modifier in effect, a single pick of an entity results in the simultaneous pick of all entities that form a contiguous chain. Entities are added to the chain so long as they meet with an entity already in the chain. This continues until there are no more unpicked entities touching the chain. Various CAD systems have different inclusion rules to determine whether the chain may grow in multiple branches, or only in a single curve.

2.1.4 Viewing Control

The fourth major aspect of the user interface is the viewing control. This control allows the user to determine how the CAD part is displayed on the screen, usually by means of a set of valuator dials. Facilities are provided to allow the user to zoom, scroll, and rotate a view of the part, and to save particular viewing states as remembered and recallable images. Zoom may be as zoom in or out by a ratio, zoom to map a digitized window to the whole screen, or a continuous zoom. Each of these allows the user to enlarge a detailed area of a drawing to facilitate work on it, and then to restore the original screen scale. Scroll is the shift of the drawing to left or right, and up or down. Scroll distance can be in discrete steps such as half the screen display, or be in a continuous motion. Scrolling is a useful method of moving to another area on a drawing while in a zoomed-in condition; the user can scroll to areas of the drawing that were not even on the original zoomed screen. Rotation is another viewing control used for three-dimensional parts. It allows the user to rotate the model so as to see it from another viewpoint. It requires the user to specify an axis of rotation and either a discrete angle of rotation, or an angular rate of rotation for continuous motion.

2.2 FILE HANDLING

All parts, designs, and programs on the CAD/CAM system are stored as files. These files are the computer's method of organizing and maintaining the large amounts of data that it deals with. The operating system of the computer allows these files to be grouped into hierarchical structures by which the CAD/CAM system administrator may sort and track work on the various parts that may be developed by users. The users need only understand the part of this hierarchy that relates to the storage and control of the part on which they work, so that they may properly retrieve it for development and file it when finished.

2.2.1 Organizing Files

The grouping of system files into hierarchical structures greatly facilitates the management of work on the CAD/CAM system. On the majority of CAD/CAM systems, this grouping is accomplished by the creation of directories. These directories can contain files, or other directories. This property of directories containing directories enables them to be linked into complex hierarchical structures. Usually, the directories are arranged into an inverted tree structure. At the base of the tree is a single directory, called the *root directory*. Other directories and subdirectories branch out from this root into a structure that is based on the working organization of the company where the system is installed. Figure 2.2 shows a hypothetical structure in a company where the CAD/CAM system is used to design and manufacture components. The root directory branches into five subdirectories: SYS contains the vendor's system software files; DEV contains subdirectories and files used by the system administrators and in-house developers; UTL contains utility programs and files available to all system users; DESIGN contains subdirectories for each design project containing the related design files; and MANUF

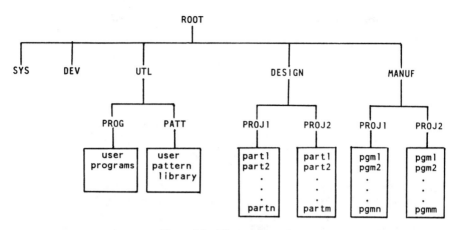

Figure 2.2   Directory hierarchy.

contains subdirectories for each manufacturing project containing the related numerical-control programs.

To specify a particular file in such a system, the user gives a pathname that describes how to reach the file when starting from the root directory. An example might be ROOT:DESIGN:PROJ1:PART2. This provides an unambiguous method of identifying each file, as simple filenames might be repeated in another directory (there is a PART2 file in the ROOT:DESIGN:PROJ2 directory also).

When doing work that requires manipulation of many files in the same directory, the constant typing of long pathnames can become unwieldy and tiresome. To help alleviate this, the concept of a working directory was developed. A working directory is a particular directory selected by the user. It can be reselected at any time. Any file in this directory can be referred to simply by its filename, without requiring the full pathname. Files that are in other directories must still be referred to by their full pathnames. The system recognizes whether a given file description is a pathname or a simple filename by noting whether the description starts with the name of the root directory. If the working directory was set to ROOT:DESIGN:PROJ1, then the file description PART2 would refer to the part in that directory. To refer to the part of the same name in the PROJ2 directory, the user would have to type the full description ROOT:DESIGN:PROJ2:PART2. Because the system detects pathnames by the presence of the root directory name, the root directory name should not be used for any other directory or filenames. Root directories are often, therefore, given unusual names such as @ or \.

Frequently, a user will want to refer to a group of files simultaneously. To provide this ability, the file management system often provides a set of wildcard characters which can be used to define criteria for including files in a group. A hypothetical set of wildcard characters and their associated meanings follows. Note that this set is more complete than the set offered by a typical CAD/CAM system.

WILDCARD CHARACTERS

```
      ?—matches any one character
      +—matches any one or more characters
      *—matches any zero or more characters
      [—matches a start of line
      ]—matches an end of line
   (a|b|c)—matches any character in the set a, b, or c
{m1|m2|m3}—matches any of the three match criteria
   & | ¬ ||—AND OR NOT XOR logical operators for combining
            criteria
```

For example, all of following would match the filename 'FRED':

```
?RED
?R?D
F*
(F|B|T)RED
+
{f+|F+}
{F*&?R*}
{?RED & ¬{BRED | TRED}}
```

while the following file description would match all of the files in the PROJ1 directories as a group:

```
ROOT:+:PROJ1:+
```

It is common practice to arrange the directories into a structure resembling the previous example. It gives a clear grouping of projects in design and engineering, projects in manufacturing, shared utilities, and files to be restricted from general access. Commonly used patterns and standard reused parts are grouped into libraries where they are easier to document and maintain, while important system files and tools still under development can be protected from general access.

2.3 FILE PROTECTION

Protecting files from unauthorized access can be easily achieved on a directory-based file management system. One common scheme involves user types and file-protection classes. Every file and directory on the system is given a protection class, and each userid is defined to be of a particular type. The user type definitions describe the types of access that users of that type may have to each of the various file-protection classes. Four types of access may be permitted. Read access allows users to see the contents of a file, or to list the contents of a directory. Files to which users do not have read access would be invisible to them. They might never know of their existence. Write access allows users to append or add data to a file, or to create new files or subdirectories in a directory. Execute access allows users to execute program files, rather than just list them. Delete access allows users to permanently delete a file or directory. Obviously, most users would be allowed only execute access to the files containing the system software, while enjoying full access to files and directories containing their own files.

A system that employs a file-protection scheme must also have a defined procedure for releasing files by changing their protection classes to a more acceptable class. The procedure can also use the connectivity of computers to aid in management tracking of release statistics by reporting the changes in protection to an administrator user. An example of such a release procedure for a system using three user types, protection classes, an electronic mail system, and an electronic engineering database might be as follows:

File Release Procedure

<Design Release>

The design work in progress is kept in the DESIGN directory with a protection class set to be invisible and inaccessible to CAM users. When a part is released to manufacturing:

- its protection class is changed to one that is available to CAM users (so they may begin using it), and visible but inaccessible to CAD users (so they may makes copies to use as a base for revisions, but not modify this version).
- a message containing the part name, a short description, and a date and time stamp is automatically generated and sent to the design manager's electronic mailbox.
- the status of the part is automatically updated in the engineering database for the project to reflect its design-released status.

<Manufacturing Release>

The manufacturing work in progress files are kept in the MANUF directory with a protection class set to be invisible and inaccessible to shop users. When a file is released to the shop:

- its protection class is changed to one that is available to shop users (so that they may begin manufacturing with it), and visible but inaccessible to CAM users (so they can also take copies for revisions).
- a message containing the part name, a short description, and a date and time stamp is automatically generated and sent to the manufacturing manager's electronic mailbox.
- the status of the part is automatically updated in the engineering database for the project to reflect its shop-released status.

2.3.1 Retrieving and Saving Files

In order to edit a text file or work on a part file, the user must first retrieve it. Retrieving causes a scratch copy of the file to be made from the version of the file stored on disk. This copy is then provided to the user. All work done by the user is actually performed on the scratch copy. When the work is completed, the user then issues a filing command which causes the scratch copy to be copied back to the disk, overwriting the old version. The scratch file is then discarded. This use of scratch files allows users to work on files, and then to later decide not to keep the changes made. In this case, the user issues a quit command which causes the scratch file to be discarded without updating the original version of the file. This leaves the original file still safe on the disk.

Most CAD/CAM systems also have a method whereby the disk version of the file can be updated to reflect changes in the scratch file, without discarding the scratch file, that is, to save the work done on the scratch copy without the exit of the part caused by a filing command. A prudent user will use this feature frequently, as power interruptions or system crashes could otherwise cause the loss of considerable amounts of work. A guideline might be to save the scratch file at least once every hour, so that a system failure can never result in more than one hour's lost work.

After retrieving a CAD part file, many systems also require the retrieval of a layout file. This layout file contains information about the particular form in which the part data will be displayed on the screen. It may control the arrangement of different views on the screen, the settings of the various view parameters. These may be the remembered values from when the part was last filed. Other systems store this information in the part file itself, together with the geometric data, and do not require this additional step to part retrieval. As the part is retrieved, it appears on the screen in a particular arrangement of views.

PROBLEMS

2.1 Entity picks that fall within the gravity field of an entity are treated as direct picks of that entity. Picks that fall outside of all gravity fields initiate a search for the nearest entity. The situation can be more complex in the cases where the pick falls within multiple gravity fields (of entities that are close together), or when the search finds several entities that are equally close to the pick location. Develop an algorithm to resolve these two cases that would be intuitive to a user and easy to implement.

2.2 Lines are considered to be "inside" a window pick if the coordinates of both endpoints fall within the window boundaries. This is not so for curves such as arcs or splines. How could you detect whether a curve is "inside" a window-pick region?

2.3 An entity can simultaneously belong to several groups, provided that those groups are nested into a hierarchy. Should it be possible to have an entity which belongs to two different distinct groups? What problems could arise in such a case?

2.4 Some file management systems allow a third structure, besides directories and files. These are "links." A link appears in a directory listing as a file but is actually a pointer to a different file in another directory. Attempts to modify or access the link file actually change the file in the other directory. When might this arrangement be useful? What dangers might also arise?

chapter 3

———

TWO DIMENSIONAL
CAD APPLICATION

3.1 OVERVIEW OF CADD

One of the earliest uses to which CAD was applied was in the field of
Computer Aided Design and Drafting (CADD). This entails the use of the
CAD system as an electronic form of the drafting table, enhanced by the
accuracy and computational power of the computer. The ability of the CAD
system to generate precise drawing graphics, combined with the power of
digital computing made for a powerful tool for a designer or draftsman. CAD
allows a user to create complex drawings with ease; libraries of subassembl-
ies and predrawn patterns are easily created and maintained, dimensioning
of engineering drawings can be automatically performed, and generation of
excellent quality plots and prints can be easily performed. Together, these
functions constitute a powerful tool to enable designers to quickly and easily
create accurate and complex designs both on paper and in an electronic form
that may be used by other computer processes. All of this begins with the
creation of a variety of entities in a CAD part file, the subject of the next
section.

3.2 CREATION OF ENTITIES

The most important function of any CAD system is its ability to create graphic entities, by which we mean points, lines, arcs, and so on. The variety of entity types that may be created, the number of methods that may be used to create them, and the ease with which they may be created are of fundamental importance in judging any CAD system. A CAD system that allows a wide variety of entity types to be created will be that much more powerful to use, and hence that much more productive. For example, the creation of a pseudo free-form curve on a system that does not allow splines is a very difficult task. The user must determine the optimum shape of the curve, and then determine how best to model that curve using numerous arcs and short line segments. The result is at best a poor approximation of a true spline curve, and an exceedingly difficult collection of entities to work with.

Similarly, a system that allows only a few methods by which a particular entity type may be constructed can be difficult and unproductive to work with. Theoretically, one method of defining a line is as good as the next. However, having a variety of methods to choose from can often result in faster construction of geometry. This is primarily due to the elimination of time spent in creating construction or temporary geometry to aid the definition of the required entity. For example, to create a line parallel to an existing line at a given distance from it, one should need only to specify the distance and the side of the original line on which to construct the new line. On a system without a "parallel at distance" method of constructing lines, this would not be the case. The construction might typically involve creating points at the endpoints of the existing line, determining a transformation matrix to translate these points to end locations of the desired line, joining the points with a line, and deleting the points.

Finally, it should also be noted that the methods of entity construction allowed should be designed to be simple, clear, and natural to the user. For example, there must be a method of defining circles that requires the user to specify only the coordinates of the center, and the radius value, as this is the most natural way to define a circle.

We now look at some of the most common entity types and their methods of definition. The accompanying figures should also be referred to.

Point.   A point is the simplest entity type that will be found on the CAD system. It is little more than a location specification with some associated graphics information and attributes. Typically, it would be displayed on the screen as a dot, small circle, or small cross. There is, therefore, a very close relation between points and location specifications. Many CAD systems allow them to be used interchangeably; the user may pick an existing point on the screen when the system would ordinarily be expecting a coordinate specification. This close relation allows a great variety of methods to be available for specifying points; every method of specifying a location may be used. As previously stated, this includes: user-entered coordinates, digitized screen positions, endpoints of entities, midpoints of entities, inter-sections between entities, specified angular locations on arcs, and nearest location on an entity.

Line.   *Point to Point:* This method of specifying a line simply involves defining a start location and an end location, either by picking point entities or by digitizing locations. The line is created from the start point to the endpoint. Many systems have a feature to this method, known as "rubber banding". With this feature, a continuously varying line is drawn from the start point to the graphics cursor, up until the endpoint is defined. Then the final line is created. "Rubber banding" refers to the fact that the continuously varying line visible during the construction appears to be a rubber band that has had one end anchored at the start point, while the other end is stretched by being attached to the graphics cursor. The specification of the endpoint is then thought of as fastening the second end of the rubber band down to the drawing.

Horizontal or Vertical: These methods are closely related to the point-to-point method. Again, the user specifies the start point by either picking a point or digitizing a location. The second point that the user indicates is used to determine the endpoint of the line—but in a different fashion. If the horizontal option is in effect, then only the x-coordinate of the second point is used to determine the endpoint of the line; the y-coordinate must necessarily be the same as the y-coordinate of the start point. Similarly for vertical lines, only the y-coordinate of the second point is used; the x-coordinate is taken from the start point. Figure 3.1 shows this and other line-creation modes. Rubber banding can also be available with these methods. The band stretches from the start point to the currently implied endpoint.

At an Angle (from the x-axis): This method creates a line at any user-specified angle from the horizontal x-axis. The line is created from a specified start point, at the given angle. The endpoint is determined by projecting from a second point, perpendicular to the line being constructed, to the line. That is to say, the line will terminate at the point closest to the second specified point. It can be seen that the horizontal and vertical methods of line specification are special cases of this more general method, where the angle from horizontal is 0 or 90 degrees, respectively. An option to create horizontal or vertical lines is usually provided, primarily to allow faster construction of these common line types.

At a Delta Angle: This method is another variant of the at-an-angle method of line construction. In this case the given angle is not measured from the horizontal x-axis, but rather is measured from another user-identified line (at an arbitrary angle). Obviously, the CAD system merely adds the angle of the other line to the angle given by the user to arrive at an angle from the x-axis value. Again, this method is provided to simplify the construction of common line types.

Parallel: Another common method of line construction is to create lines parallel to each other separated by specific distances. An option is usually provided to accomplish this, in which the user identifies the line he or she wishes to create a parallel to, the side on which the parallel is to be constructed, and the distance by

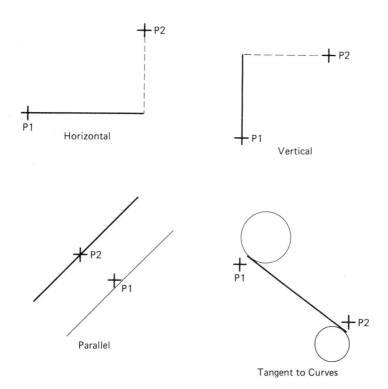

Figure 3.1   Line-creation options.

which the new line is to be separated from the original line. The distance can be specified either by entering a numerical value or by digitizing a location through which the parallel must pass.

Perpendicular: Lines may also be created that are perpendicular to another entity. Note that the other entity does not have to be a line; it can also be a circle, or conic, or spline curve. The user identifies the entity that he or she wishes to create a perpendicular line to, and then digitizes a point somewhere off of that entity. A line is then created which goes from the digitized location to a point on the selected entity. The particular point used on the entity will be chosen so that the line created is perpendicular to the entity at that location (this point will always be the location on the entity that is closest to the digitized location).

Tangent to Two Curves: A powerful method of line construction is to create lines which lie smoothly tangent to existing curves (circles, conics, splines). The user simply specifies the two curves that the line should be tangent to. The approximate locations of the points of tangency must also be specified. This is to resolve the ambiguity in choosing a tangency point. Each circle or conic has two points of tangency that can be used in any particular specification; splines may have a large (potentially infinite) number.

Through a Point, Tangent to a Curve: This is a variant of the previous method, in which a line is constructed tangent to a specified curve and through a specified point. Essentially, the point is treated as a circle of zero radius, and a line is constructed between the two curves as previously discussed.

Circle.   *Center and Radius:* The most common method of creating circles is by specifying a location for the center of the circle and a value for the radius. The radius may be given either by a numerical value or by digitizing a location that must lie on the circumference of the circle (the radius then being the minimum distance between that location and the center). Figure 3.2 shows the circle-creation modes.

Diameter: A circle may also be specified by specifying two points that lie on the diameter of the circle.

Three Points: Another method is to specify three points that, while not lying on the diameter of the circle, do lie on the circumference. A unique circle is then defined. This method is very useful when the user is attempting to smooth an arbitrary circle through known locations, as neither the center location nor the radius value need be known in advance.

Two Points and Bulge: This fairly uncommon method of circle specification uses two points that lie on the circumference of the desired circle. The bulge value indicates the maximum distance that the circle arcs away from the chord joining the two points (see accompanying Figure 3.2 for an example).

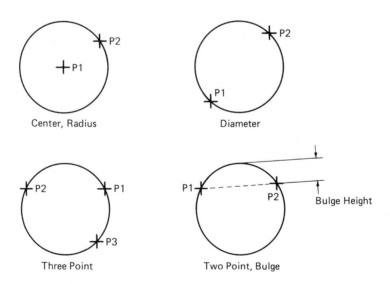

Figure 3.2   Circle-creation options.

Arc.   Arcs are very similar entities to circles. They differ only in that arcs have definite start points and endpoints. In fact, many CAD systems do not distinguish between circles and arcs; they treat circles as arcs with coincident start points and endpoints. The start and end specifications of arcs are usually given as angles measured counterclockwise from the *x*-axis, with the start point occurring first. Thus, arcs are considered to have a counterclockwise sense, or direction, to them. All of the methods of defining circles are also applicable to arcs. Arcs simply require the additional specification of their starts and ends. There are two methods to do this.

Points: These points may lie on or off the circumference of the arc. Points that lie on the circumference serve as start points or endpoints. Points that do not lie on the circumference can be used to imply start points or endpoints. The CAD system does this by considering a line from the arc center to the specified point. Where this hypothetical line would intersect the circumference of the arc is then used as the start point or endpoint of the arc.

Angles: Alternatively, the start or end may be specified by explicitly entering a numeric angular value, from the horizontal.

Fillet.   Strictly speaking, a fillet is no different than an arc; it is circular and has distinct start and end positions. It has been granted separate status because its uses and its construction methods are considerably different than typical arcs. A fillet is an arc that smoothly blends between entities. The most common application is in rounding off sharp corners between two lines. The fillet arc is constructed such that it lies tangent to the entities. These entities, while most often lines, can also be any type of curve.

Fillet creation usually has an additional option to specify whether the entities being filleted should be trimmed to their new points of tangency with the fillet, or whether they should be left untrimmed. One, both, or none may be trimmed in this way.

Two Entities and Radius: In this method of fillet construction, the user picks the two entities to be filleted and specifies a value of the radius desired. The CAD system then constructs an arc of the desired radius, located such that it is tangent to both of the entities, starting at the first tangency point, and ending at the second tangency point.

There are several potential ambiguities to this method. First, the method fails to construct anything if it is impossible to create a fillet of the desired radius, tangent to the entities. Second, there may be multiple tangency points on an entity, if the entity is a curve. Circles and arcs often have two points that satisfy the tangency and radius constraints; splines often have a great number. This ambiguity is resolved by the system by noting where on the curve the user picked to identify it. The potential tangency point that lies closest to this location is used (see Figure 3.3). The user must also be aware that the fillet is constructed with the normal counterclockwise sense of arcs. Thus, the portion of the arc that is actually displayed is that portion that runs counterclockwise from the start point to the endpoint.

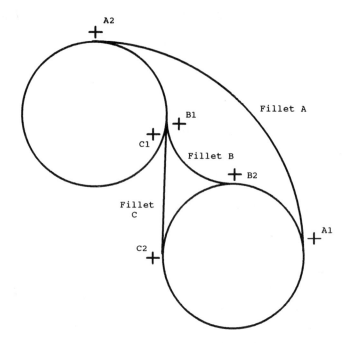

Figure 3.3   Fillet-creation option.

Three Entities: This method closely follows the three-point method of arc construction. The user picks three entities, again taking care to digitize close to the desired points of tangency. The CAD system then constructs an arc of the necessary radius, from the first tangency point, through the second, and ending at the third tangency point.

Conics.   Conics allow the user to create curves such as ellipses, parabolas, and hyperbolas. For ellipses, the user digitizes a center location and specifies, either through numeric values or digitizes, a length for the major axis, a length for the minor axis, a rotation angle from horizontal, and optional start and end angles for the curve. Parabolas can be created by specifying a focus location, a line to serve as a directrix, and maximum values for the length of the arms. Hyperbolas can be defined by pairs of intersecting lines and a focus value.

Five Points: All conics can also be specified by digitizing five locations, or points. All different conic types, including circles, can be created by judicious placement of these points. This method of construction is commonly used to create smooth curves that pass through up to five specified locations.

Coefficients: A less common method of specifying conics is to explicitly give the five coefficients of the generalized equation for a conic $Ax^2 + Bx + Cxy + Dy + Ey^2 + F = 0$. This form of specification is known as *canonical form,* and most closely resembles the form in which the conic information is stored by the CAD system.

String.   A string is a series of locations that are joined by line segments. All of these line segments are collectively treated as a single entity. There are two different methods to define a string, which on some CAD systems can be intermixed during the string definition. The first is to pick points or digitize locations. The string is constructed to join these locations. The second is to pick existing lines. The string segments will line on top of these lines, with their lengths either increased or decreased to meet the next segment at their common intersection point.

Centerlines.   *Through Locations:* This type of centerline is created by digitizing two or more locations that the centerline is to pass through. The locations chosen must be collinear to allow the construction of a straight line between them.

Circles: The user picks a single circle or arc. A centerline is constructed through the center of the circle and extending slightly beyond its diameter.

Bolt Circles: This method is very similar to the through-locations method, differing only in that the locations chosen must lie on a single circular arc. The system then creates a bolt circle through them.

Axis: In this method, the user identifies a start point and an endpoint to define a cylindrical axis. A centerline is then constructed between these locations. This method is not found on many CAD systems, as it is identical to a simple point-to-point line creation. On those systems, the user would simply create a line using a centerline line font.

Vector.   A vector is similar to a line. It has an associated direction from start point to endpoint, and an associated magnitude equivalent to its length. It differs from a line in that it cannot be trimmed or operated on, it cannot be used to define locations by intersection or by endpoint, and it often does not have any graphical representation on the screen. It can usually be created only by explicit coordinate entry or by location digitizing. Its primary purpose is to represent translation directions and distances for use in transforming or offsetting entities.

Text.   Text entities are used to create notes in the part. To create text, the user must typically specify the contents of the text, the location in the part to place the text (this location will usually be mapped to the lower left corner of the first line of text, but this can be modified as we shall see), and a number of parameters that define the style and size of the text.

Symbol.   Symbols are closely related to text and in many CAD systems are simply considered as a particular text font. Some special symbols that may be available on a CAD system are: ° ± ∇ (f) (r) (m). They are added to a part by specifying the symbol type, and by digitizing the location where it is to be placed.

Group.   Entity groups are created simply by picking the entities that are to be included in the group. As explained in Chapter 2, the group can usually contain other group entities, thus creating a hierarchy of groups. A group itself is selected by picking an entity that is contained in the group. In CAD systems that allow nesting of group structures, picking an entity might result in an ambiguity as to which level of group was intended to be selected. This can be resolved by either of two methods. There may be a default level of selection, such as "first group level above individual entities," that is always taken. On more sophisticated systems, there is a function that allows the user to override the default and force the selection, repeatedly, one level higher or lower.

Spline.   A spline is a smooth free-form curve whose shape is controlled by a number of user-defined points or locations. In many applications it is an essential entity type to be provided by the system, although several smaller CAD systems lack it. This lack can be attributed to the data storage and computational resources required to handle splines; they are considerably more complex entities for the system to manipulate than are lines or arcs. Besides their associated control points, splines have definite start points and endpoints, a directional sense (from start to end), and an associated parameter u which varies uniformly from 0 to 1 over the length of the spline. This parameter is used by the system to aid its manipulations of the spline, and on some systems is also available to the user for various purposes such as specifying a point at a specific u-value point along a spline.

An important concept in dealing with high-order curves such as splines is mathematical continuity. Zero-order continuity refers to whether individual splines have breaks or sudden location discontinuities, or whether pairs of splines that are meant to meet at a common point do meet. All CAD systems allow the user to have control over the endpoints of splines, thereby insuring zero-order continuity. First-order continuity refers to the slope of splines. Individual splines without first-order continuity will exhibit cusp points which may not be desirable; pairs of meeting splines that do not have first-order continuity will exhibit sharp corners at their meeting point. Most CAD systems create splines with first-order continuity assured, and provide functions that modify the slope of a spline at its endpoints so that first-order continuity between splines can be achieved. Second-order continuity then refers to the curvature of splines. Some CAD systems provide functions to modify the curvature of splines at their endpoints, so that second-order continuity between splines can be achieved. However, such modifications to the second derivative of a curve can cause serious distortions in the shape of the curve, and so must be employed with caution. Three different methods of creating splines are commonly employed. They will be considered in turn.

Hermite Splines: These splines are defined by start points and endpoints, and start and end vectors. The shape of the spline is controlled by the direction and magnitude of the vectors. Figure 3.4 shows the effect of varying the magnitude of the start vector, while Figure 3.5 shows the effect of varying its direction.

Bezier Splines: These splines are similar to the Hermite splines, except that the end vectors are implied by two additional points that do not lie on the spline. The four defining points create a so-called convex-hull region inside of which the spline is guaranteed to lie. This is an important aid to users, as they can easily visualize how a change in a defining point may affect the shape of the spline.

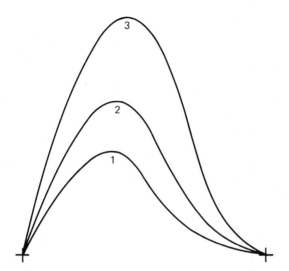

Figure 3.4   Hermite spline magnitude effect.

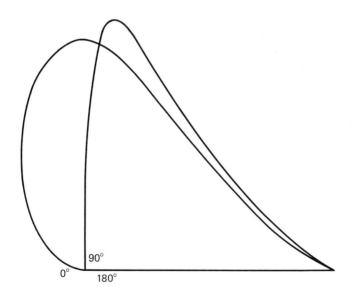

Figure 3.5   Hermite spline direction effect.

Higher-order Bezier splines may also be created, where several points on the interior of the spline may also control its shape. Figure 3.6 shows a fourth-order spline whose shape is controlled by five points. Bezier splines do not necessarily pass through any but the start point and endpoint, which makes them somewhat difficult to control. However, this same property makes them very smooth and visually appealing, which has its particular design applications.

The relationship between the placement of the nonendpoints of a Bezier spline and the shape of the resulting curve can be difficult for a designer to predict. This is because the placement of an individual control point affects the shape of the entire spline. In this way, the Bezier spline is said to have global blending functions. Figure 3.7 shows the weight with which the placement of individual points affects the shape of the curve for a fourth-order spline.

B-splines: B-splines are usually used in higher-order forms. They provide second-order continuity to the user by not necessarily passing through any of their control points, including the endpoints. They also differ from Bezier splines in that their blending functions are local, as illustrated in Figure 3.8. This makes them somewhat easier to control by judicious placement of their control points, although they lack the graceful smoothness of Bezier splines.

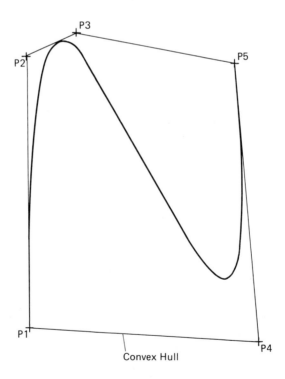

Figure 3.6   Five-point bezier spline

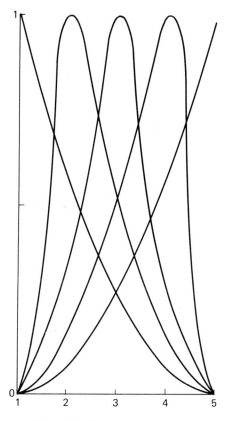

Figure 3.7   Global blending functions.

3.2.1 Attributes

Attributes are those pieces of information associated with entities or CAD parts that are not connected to the definition of geometry or entities. They are used to store information in a textual form, in the part itself, where it is necessarily readily available to anyone working with the part. Attributes may also store information about the part itself, such as library inclusion information, or revision history, or part version control information. This information is then stored with the part in a form that is easily accessible to the user for reference. Such attributes are called part attributes and may be accessed by specifying the part name.

Attributes may also be associated to particular entities, storing additional information relevant to that particular entity only. These entity attributes can be accessed by picking the entity itself. Entity attributes may store information about when an entity was created, or a history of modifications made to it, or parametric data of the entity.

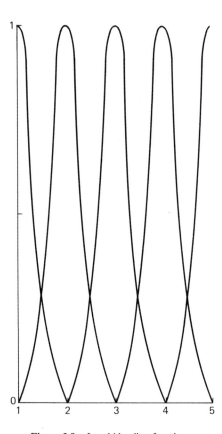

Figure 3.8   Local blending functions.

Both part attributes and entity attributes may often be augmented by additional user-defined attributes. Typically user attributes are created by first creating an attribute type of a given tag name, such as "Size." Then, that attribute is associated to a chosen entity and given a particular value for this entity, such as "25 mm."

The fact that different entities may have different values for a particular attribute is exploited by some CAD systems to give the user a new method of selection. This selection by attribute value may be used to pick entities (by creating an attribute tag NAME associated to all entities, and then masking the pick to select only entities with the NAME attribute set to "LINE 1," for example), or to control group level selection (by creating an attribute tag GRP_LEVEL, and then picking a particular group in the hierarchy by masking for GRP_LEVEL to be set to 2, for example), or for identifying special entities in retrieved part figures (see Section 3.2.3) or identifying entities created by programs (see Chapter 5). If these entities are originally created with particular values for an attribute, they can later be individually identified by another user when added to his or her part by one of these two methods.

Layers

Layers are a special type of attribute shared by all entities except groups. They can be visualized as a number of clear sheets or overlays on which entities are drawn. These sheets can be added or removed from the drawing at any time to aid in the visualization of complex parts or assembly drawings. A layer can be in any of four different states at a particular time:

1. *WorkLayer*   This is the layer on which newly created entities are placed. Only one layer can be designated as the work layer at any time.
2. *Active*   Layers with this status are visible and accessible to the user. Entities on these layers can be seen, manipulated, and used to define locations.
3. *Reference*   Layers with this status are visible but inaccessible. This means that the entities on these layers can be seen by the user but are being ignored by the system. This is useful in displaying entities, while protecting them from accidental deletion or modification.
4. *Inactive*   These layers are not visible. The entities on them are not visible to the user, nor can they be accessed or modified.

Many systems allow layers to be used as an additional method of masking entity picks. For example, users may wish to restrict their entity picks to lines that are on layer 5.

Discriminations

Discriminations are also special types of attributes. They control the way in which entities appear when displayed on the screen, and thus help the user to discriminate between entities on display.

Color is used as an attribute to discriminate entities. Individual entities may be assigned various colors to help the user to group them logically. For example, all entities forming a particular subassembly in a part may be displayed in green. Some CAD systems have only monochromatic CRTs and cannot display color as a discrimination, while others may allow from two to several thousand different colors to be simultaneously displayed. Some systems allow only a dozen different colors to be used but compensate by allowing the user to select those active colors from a palette of several thousand colors.

The line font, or style, that entities are displayed in is also used to discriminate. Typically, a CAD system will allow line fonts of solid, dashed, phantom, and centerline. Some systems allow many more line fonts, and may even allow the user to define new line fonts.

Another form of discrimination is density, or line weight. Entities may be assigned densities of thin, medium, thick, or a numerical value. This variation may appear on the screen as a variation in line width, or a variation in brightness. On plots, this variation appears as line thickness.

Like layers, discriminations may also be allowed as additional masks for entity selection. For example, selection may be restricted to entities that are thin dashed lines on layer 5. It may also be possible to nest these attributes so that different layers have different default discriminations. In such a case the system could be set so that different layers appear in different colors, or other combinations.

Finally, there is the type of discrimination that is used by the system to indicate picked entities. This is known as highlighting and may be achieved by use of a special color, or line font, or by causing the highlighted entity to blink on and off. Some systems allow users to place entities in this highlighted, or picked, state without actually modifying them. This can be used as a temporary way of emphasizing certain entities during the construction process.

3.2.2 Drafting Entities

These following entity types are commonly used in the creation of finished drawings, and so belong in the realm of computer-aided drafting only. Their primary purpose is to convey information to anyone using the plot of a finished drawing. Like dimensions, some are actually redundant or potentially misleading if the electronic version of the part is to be used later in the manufacturing process. In such a case, textual information is best stored as an attribute, while dimensional data can be extracted directly from the geometry. The continuing use of CAD systems as electronic drafting machines, or for the creation of technical drawings, provides a continuing use for these drafting entities.

Notes

Notes are isolated text entities that serve to add information to a drawing. As mentioned previously, they are created by digitizing an origin and supplying text to be displayed. The style in which the text is displayed is governed by a number of parameters that can be set by the user. The most common of these text parameters are:

Case   This governs whether text is displayed in mixed case, or in upper case only.

Justification   For notes containing several lines of text, this parameter controls whether those lines should be adjusted to align on the left, on the right, or to be equispaced about the center of the note.

Font   Most CAD systems allow the user to select which of several fonts the letters will be displayed in. Some systems allow users to create their own custom character fonts, although this can be an arduous task. Provisions may also be made to display text in a fast font, or a box font. These are temporary fonts that are used to speed up the display of text on the screen; characters may at any time be switched from these fonts to a regular font. Fast fonts are simple stick letters designed to be quickly drawn by the CRT screen. Box fonts are simple rectangular boxes that replace an entire note. They are much faster for the system to draw and therefore make zooms and such much faster on parts containing many notes.

Height   This parameter controls the height (either in millimeters or inches) of characters.

Width/Proportion   This parameter governs the width of characters independently of their height, and so controls their proportion or aspect ratio.

Proportional Spacing   A yes/no type parameter that determines whether intercharacter spacing will be constant or proportional to the character's width.

Text Angle   This parameter, specified in degrees, controls the angle at which individual lines of text run from horizontal. A variation on this is to allow the user to specify a line or curve that the text is to run along. The text angle is then varied to suit.

Character Slant   The ability to slant characters allows for the creation of italics or other effects. This parameter controls the angle that characters will slant from vertical.

Character Rotation   Individual characters may be rotated about their origins. Combined with a text angle of 90 degrees, this allows the user to create vertical writing in notes.

Origin Site   As previously stated, the bottom left corner of the first line in a note is usually mapped to the location digitized by the user. Sometimes this does not provide sufficient control over the placement of the note. In these cases the origin site of the note can be moved from its lower left position to another position. Other permissible positions may be the middle or right of the first line, the left or middle or right of the last line, or the exact center of the note.

Some systems also provide certain control codes that can be imbedded into text to affect its appearance when displayed. Some codes may produce boxes around the text, such as those used for geometric tolerancing or feature control symbols in drafting. Some may produce special symbols that are not normally part of the selected character font. Some may also effect inline parameter changes, so that certain words in the text may be emphasized by different character sizes, fonts, or slants.

Labels

Like notes, labels are text entities that additionally have leaders or arrows originating with them and pointing to another part of the drawing. They share all of the text parameters that notes have, while additionally having these parameters to control the appearance of the leader:

Leader Side   This parameter controls whether the leader will emerge from the left or right side of the label text.

Leader Tail   The leader may start directly at an angle towards its destination point, or may begin with a short horizontal segment. The user is allowed to vary the length of this tail (down to zero if desired).

Arrow Type   An option may be provided to vary the style of arrowhead with which the leader terminates. Typically the user may choose closed arrowheads, open arrowheads, dots, slashes, or no arrowhead at all.

Leader Top/Bot   Another parameter controls whether the leader originates from the first or last line of the label text.

Associativity   The concept of associativity is covered in Section 3.2.5 more completely. Suffice to say that this parameter determines whether the tip of the leader becomes "fastened" to an entity that it points to, and thereby "follows" it should that entity be moved in the part.

Dimensions

There is a great variety of dimension types available on CAD systems and a great number of associated parameters to control their format and appearance. Some parameters apply to all dimension types, while others pertain to certain types only.

There are eight primary types of dimensions that are found on most CAD systems. These can be grouped into three classes: linear, radial, and angular. Linear dimensions comprise five different dimension types. The first is the horizontal dimension, which gives the horizontal measure between two locations in the part. These locations do not necessarily have to be in horizontal alignment with each other. The dimension will give only the horizontal component of the distance between them. Vertical dimensions likewise give the vertical distance between different locations. Parallel dimensions are used to give the true dimension between points, measured parallel to the straight line between them. Perpendicular dimensions, as implied by their name, give the distance from a location to an entity as measured perpendicularly to the entity. Finally, ordinate dimensions are used to give successive distances from a particular datum line. In Figure 3.9, each of the different types of linear dimension can be seen. Radial dimensions are used to give radial information about circles and arcs. Only two types are available: radial and diametrical. Finally, there is an angular dimension for giving measure of included angles between entities.

The parameters that govern the display of dimensions can be divided into those that affect the format of the total dimension, those that affect the format of the dimension text, and those that affect the measure of the dimension

Arrow Type   Like labels, dimensions can have various styles of arrowheads.

Arrow Size   The size of the arrowhead, relative to the text of the dimension, can often be controlled by the user.

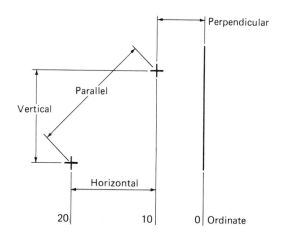

Figure 3.9   Linear dimensions.

Arrow Location   This parameter contrils the placement of arrows and dimension lines, relative to the witness lines. When set to inside, the system will always place them between the witness lines for nonradial dinensions and on the inside of arcs for radical dimensions. Likewise, when set to outside, they will always appear outside of the witness lines or arcs. When set to automatic, however, the system will calculate the size of the dimension text string and then determine wheter they can fit inside. If not, they are placed outside.

Text Location   This parameter controls the placement of the dimension text within the dimension. When set to automatic, the system strives to place it centered between the witness lines. If there is not adequate room, the system will place the text outside, either to the left or right of the witness lines as it determines the more appropriate. When this parameter is set to align, the system also strives to place the dimension in alignment with another user-identified dimension. When set to manual, the text is placed exactly where digitized by the user, without regard to spacing.

Appended Text Location   Appended text refers to additional user-entered text, such as "REF" or "TYP," that is to be included with the dimensions text. This parameter controls the placement of this text relative to the main text: either before, after, above, or below.

Text Orientation   The dimension text may either appear aligned with the direction of the dimension line, or always appear horizontal.

Dimension Line   The dimension line may be either solid (with the text appearing above it), or broken (with the text placed in the gap).

Text Gap   For broken dimension lines, this parameter controls the size of the gap between the dimension line and the text.

Witness Line Gap   This controls the size of the gap between the witness line and the associated location or geometry.

Text Parameters   All of the parameters for controlling the appearance of text in notes and labels are usually available for controlling the appearance of dimension text.

Leading Zero   The leading zero of dimensions that are decimals less than one may optionally be suppressed.

Decimal Point   In many countries, a comma is used as a decimal point, while in North America a period is used. This parameter allows the user to choose which form will be used for dimensions in the CAD part.

Diameter Symbol   This allows the user to specify what symbol will be added to the dimension text to specify diameters (Ø, DIA). It also determines whether the symbol will precede or follow the main text.

Radius Symbol   Likewise, the user can select the symbol (R , RAD) to indicate a radial dimension, and its placement.

Units   The units in which dimensions are calculated and displayed may be selected by the user. Typical choices might be meters, centimeters, millimeters, feet, feet and inches, decimal inches, or fractional inches.

Precision   For decimally represented units, precision controls the number of decimal places that are displayed in the dimension. For fractionally represented dimensions, it determines the smallest unit of resolution permitted (such as 1/16). Dimensions are rounded to this precision if necessary.

Angular Units   Angular dimensions are usually measured in degrees, but may also be represented in radians or as a gradient of a particular percentage of a right angle. This parameter allows the user the choice.

Angular Precision   As for linear precision, this parameter controls the number of decimal places for decimally represented values. It may also allow the user to specify angles in degree-minute, or degree-minute-second form.

Scale Factor   A scale factor is used when geometry has been drawn to a different scale than the actual part it may represent. The CAD system calculates the actual distance between the dimension locations, and then multiplies this value by the scale factor before displaying it as the dimension text.

Tolerance   This parameter allows for the automatic inclusion of tolerance text. The user would specify whether the tolerance is shown as unidirectional or bi-directional appended text, or as maximum and minimum values of the main text.

Dual Dimension   Occasionally, a user may wish to show dimensions in two units simultaneously (such as millimeters and inches). There are parameters to control this dual dimensioning, including the units of the dual text, its location relative to the primary text, its precision and tolerance, and whether the dual text is to be enclosed in brackets.

Associativity   Like labels, dimensions may also be associated or bound to geometry. In the case of dimensions, this has the effect of having the dimension text dynamically reflect the distance between two entities. If one of the entities should be moved, the dimension would be automatically regenerated with the new distance as its text.

Crosshatching

Crosshatching is a method of filling in bounded areas in a drawing to help clarify complex geometry. It is specified by picking the entities that constitute the border of the region. There are four main parameters to the creation of crosshatching.

Style   This refers to the pattern with which the area is filled. There are several standard patterns that are used to indicate the material from which a part is to be made. Figure 3.10 shows some of these patterns.

Spacing   The spacing between successive lines in the crosshatch pattern can be set by this parameter.

Angle   This parameter is used to set the angle from horizontal that the pattern is drawn at. It is often preset to 45 degrees.

Associativity   The crosshatching entity may be associated to its boundary entities so that it will be regenerated to reflect any changes in their placement.

3.2.3 Figures

Figures are a method of saving the time needed to create repetitive geometry in many different part files. They provide a way of creating the repeated geometry once, and then allowing it to be copied into several other files. The figure geometry is kept in a separate file on the system that may be retrieved or copied into any part file. The user creates a figure from geometry in a part by picking the geometry and entering a name for the figure file. The system then creates a figure file and copies the selected geometry into it.

Two distinct sorts of figures can exist, with quite different properties. The first is the part figure. When a part figure is retrieved into a file, copies of the figure entities are added to the file. These entities thereafter behave exactly as any other entities in the part, and may be treated identically. In retrieving them, the user may opt to have them automatically placed in a group and to have them all placed on the work layer (they may have been on different layers in the figure file). The part figure file itself is very much like a normal part file. In fact, in many systems it is identical; all parts files may be treated as figures.

The second type of figure, the pattern figure, is a more complex arrangement. When a pattern figure is retrieved, no geometric entities are actually added to the part file. Instead a type of pointer entity, called an instance, is added at the location where the figure is desired. This instance directs the CAD system to display at this

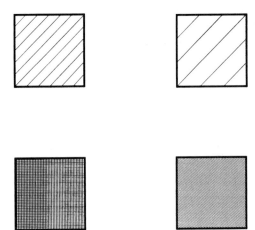

Figure 3.10 Crosshatch patterns

location the contents of the figure file named by the instance. The resulting entities
that are displayed to the user are not actually in the part and are not pickable. They
act as if permanently on reference layers. The instance itself is a pickable entity,
which allows the pattern figure to be deleted or transformed.

3.2.4 Nodal Entities

Nodal entities are similar to the entities discussed previously. They differ
only in that they are not fully specified or complete when added to the drawing;
they contain nodes or empty slots where the remaining defining information is to
be inserted. This information may be specific parameter values dependent on the
entity type or, in the case of textual nodal entities, the text itself. That is to say that
a nodal note could be created in a part, with all of the text parameters set to give a
particular appearance, but with no text to display. Several of these entities could
be placed in the part, all awaiting text. The user could then, at a later time, enter
text for each nodal note. This text would then be displayed at the location of the
node, with the text parameters of the node.

This process of supplying information to a node is called *instantiating* the
nodal entity. Each note thus created would be an instance of the nodal note.
One obvious application of this is in the creation of text-containing figures,
where the text varies with the figure application. The creator of the figure would
place nodal notes in the figure at the correct locations and with the correct text
parameters to suit the layout of the rest of the figure. Another user could then
retrieve this figure and simply instantiate the notes by entering the text without
concern for its placement or appearance. The notes would then appear in the
figure with the correct placement and parameters as selected by the original
creator of the figure. A standard drawing title block is an excellent example
application of this method.

3.2.5 Associativity

Associativity is a method by which different CAD entities can be related in a dynamic fashion. In the description of the entity being associated is a pointer to another entity. Certain information is taken from this second entity and used in the determination of the current entity.

In the case of labels, the label is associated to a geometric entity. Positional information is then taken from that geometric entity and used to control the placement of the tip of the label leader. In this manner, the leader appears to be attached to the entity and will change in angle and length to accommodate any changes in the geometric entity.

For dimensions, the associated geometry provides more information still. The witness lines and the dimension line are positionally determined by the location of the entities being dimensioned so that, should the entities be moved, the dimension will stretch or shrink accordingly. Also, the dimension text is dynamically calculated from these positions each time that the dimension is displayed on the screen. This allows the dimension text to be automatically updated during modifications of the geometry. Contrast this to nonassociative dimensions, where the text is calculated once and then permanently displayed as the dimension text. When the geometry changes, this type of dimension must be deleted and recreated.

This associativity can also be applied at the level of actual files on the CAD system. As can be seen from the previous discussion of pattern figures, they are necessarily associative entities. Any changes to the figure file are automatically reflected in parts that have instances of the figure. Also, in some systems part figures are added to parts in an associative manner, so that any changes to the original figure file will automatically be reflected in any parts that use that part figure. This associativity creates a "live" database of interconnected parts that can dynamically reflect changes in any area of the database.

3.3 ENTITY MANIPULATION

The following four sets of functions provide methods by which entities may be manipulated. The first set deals with the removal of entities from the part. The second set is for the modification of an entity's defining parameters. The third set deals with the graphical appearance of entities, while the final set is for the application of geometric transformations to entities.

Entity Deletion

Delete   This command removes an entity from the part. The graphics disappear from the screen, and the entity and its attributes are no longer known to the system. Typically, the defining data are still contained in the part file, they are just marked as inaccessible. This feature allows for the existence of the next function.

Undelete   This command restores a deleted entity to the part. The entity reappears on the screen and can be accessed. This is very useful as an "oops" function to restore accidentally deleted entities that may have been very difficult to create in their particular form. Some systems track only the most recently deleted entity as a possible candidate for undeletion, while others will allow the user to successively undelete all entities that have been deleted.

Pack File   Since deleted entities are not actually removed from the part file, part files can grow to be inordinately large and bulky if much creation and deletion of entities are done. Most CAD systems have a method of permanently removing deleted entities from the file and thereby regaining that storage space. A pack file command is sometimes provided to perform this function. Alternatively, this process may occur automatically every time that a part is filed back to the disk. Once a part is packed in this way, all previously deleted entities are permanently gone. No information about them is retained in the part.

Parameter Changing

Edit Entity   This command provides the user with a method of modifying parameters that affect the entity in a relatively minor fashion. Changes such as repositioning a spline point or changing the font of a line can be done in this way without requiring the user to create a new entity with the desired features.

Change Entity   Major changes in the defining information of an entity can be accomplished with this command. It allows the user to make changes such as the radius of an arc, or the number of points in a spline.

Graphics Manipulation

Blank Entity   This command has the effect of temporarily making an entity unpickable and removing its graphics from the screen. It is as if the entity had been moved to an inactive layer. This is useful in temporarily uncluttering a portion of a part, without deactivating entire layers. An unblanking command is usually also provided to restore all blanked entities to their normal status.

Blank/Font in View   A variation on the blank command is to blank an entity, or change its font in a single view. The entity would keep its normal appearance in all other views. Views and view-related commands are primarily used in 3D CAD applications and are treated more in Chapter 4.

Interval Blanking/Fonting   Another occasionally useful variation on this theme is to blank, or change the font of, only a portion of the entity. The indicated portion would be blanked, while the remainder of the entity is left unchanged.

Transformations

A powerful set of commands on any CAD system is the set of transformations. These commands allow the user to move, rotate, and change the size of any geometry in a part without having to recreate new geometry of a different location, orientation, or size. These transformations can be of four different types.

Translate.   This transformation causes picked geometry to be moved to a new location in the part. Its orientation and scale is not changed. The distance and direction of the move can be specified in may ways. The user may pick a vector entity, a vector may be implicitly defined by digitizing a "from" location and a "to" location; the vector may be implicitly specified by entering its components, or the geometry may be dragged. Dragging is equivalent to the from/to method with rubber banding added. The user specifies a from point, which is then continuously mapped to the graphics cursor position. The entities picked for translation dynamically follow the cursor until a to point is digitized. At that time the entities become permanently positioned in their new locations.

A useful option to the translate transformation is to have any adjoining entities stretch, so that they remain in contact with the translated entities. In stretching, these entities would have some of their defining coordinates also translated to insure that they remain adjoining.

Rotate.   This transformation causes the picked geometry to be rotated about a specified axis through a specified angle. In 2D CAD, the axis is assumed to be perpendicular to the plane of the screen, passing through a location digitized by the user. In 3D CAD, the axis may be specified by picking a line or by digitizing two locations to indicate the poles of the axis. The angle part of the specification may either be entered as a value in degrees, or implied by digitizing approximate start and end locations on a plane perpendicular to the axis.

Scale.   The scaling transformation changes the size of picked geometry. The user must enter a scaling factor and then digitize a location to serve as a scaling origin. Entities are scaled by determining, for all points on the entity, the distance from the scaling origin. This distance is multiplied by the scale factor, and the point is then translated by the difference. Obviously, short cuts are used wherever possible. These include moving only the endpoints of a line and then redrawing the line, and moving only the origin of an arc and redrawing with a scaled radius value.

With more powerful CAD systems, separate scale factors can be specified for the different coordinate axis; an entity may be scaled by a factor of 2 in the y-direction, and a factor of 0.5 in the x-direction. In this way, entities can be stretched or distorted as required.

Mirror.   This transformation causes the picked geometry to be transformed as if reflected through an imaginary mirror. The position of the virtual mirror is specified by the user. In 2D cases, the mirror is considered to be perpendicular to the plane of the screen, intersecting it in a line. The user may therefore pick an existing line entity, or digitize two locations that imply a line, to describe the mirror position. In 3D cases, two lines or three noncollinear points are necessary to define the mirror plane.

The action of the mirror transformation is actually a special case of an axis-independent scale transformation. For instance, a reflection through a mirror that intersects the screen through the y-axis is actually a scale transformation with a y-scale of 1 and an x-scale of -1. The -1 x-scale causes points that were a given distance to the right of the y-axis mirror to be moved to the equivalent distance left of the mirror. In this way, an entity that did move away from the mirror to the right will now move away to the left and will be on the opposite side of the mirror.

There is one option of transformation that applies to all of these functions: the copy option. By choosing this option, the user can direct the transformation to be performed not on the picked entities, but on identical copies of them. The result is to have two sets of entities, the unchanged originals and the transformed copies. These copies may or may not have an associativity with the originals, such that changes in the originals also occur to the copies. This depends on the particular CAD system being used.

The concept of transforming copies can be augmented in two manners. First, the user might specify a repetition factor that would cause the transformation of copies process to be applied repeatedly to the copies themselves, thereby creating a series of copies. Alternatively, an array of transformed copies could be created, if the transformation were a translation. This array could be either a rectangular array in which the user would specify the horizontal and vertical spacings of the copies, or a circular array in which the user would specify the radius and angular separation of the copies. Figure 3.11 shows examples of each of the transformation types, while Figure 3.12 shows the effects of a copy option. Note the difference between a repetitive copy of a rotation and a circular array of a translation.

As mentioned, entities are transformed by transforming the defining points of them. To transform points, the coordinates of the point are expressed as a vector. This vector is multiplied with a transformation matrix to yield a vector of the new coordinates of the point. There are three forms that this transformation matrix can take:

Translation:

$$\begin{vmatrix} 1 & 0 & 0 \\ 0 & 1 & 0 \\ dx & dy & 1 \end{vmatrix}$$ where dx, dy are the x and y displacements.

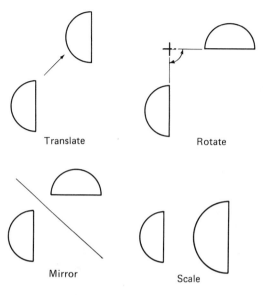

Translate   Rotate

Mirror   Scale

Figure 3.11   Transformations.

Rotation about the origin:

$$\begin{vmatrix} \cos\theta & -\sin\theta & 0 \\ \sin\theta & \cos\theta & 0 \\ 0 & 0 & 1 \end{vmatrix}$$ where θ is the angle of rotation

Note that this is for rotations about the origin $(x,y) = (0,0)$. Rotations about other points are actually combinations of rotations about the origin and translations.
Scale:

$$\begin{vmatrix} Sx & 0 & 0 \\ 0 & Sy & 0 \\ 0 & 0 & 1 \end{vmatrix}$$ where Sx, Sy are the x and y scale factors

Because these are 3×3 matrices, the point vectors must have three elements. They are therefore described as:

$$\begin{vmatrix} x \\ y \\ 1 \end{vmatrix}$$

Chapter 4 introduces three-dimensional CAD entities and modeling. It is useful to note here that these transformation matrices can be easily generalized to the 3D case, as follows:

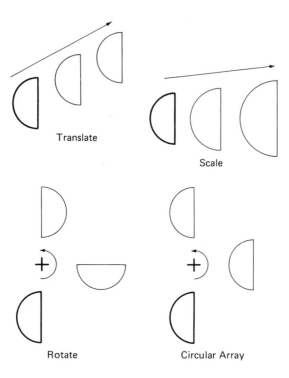

Figure 3.12 Transformation with copy option.

Translation:

$$\begin{vmatrix} 1 & 0 & 0 & 0 \\ 0 & 1 & 0 & 0 \\ 0 & 0 & 1 & 0 \\ dx & dy & dz & 1 \end{vmatrix}$$

Rotation about the origin:

$$\begin{vmatrix} \cos\theta & -\sin\theta & 0 & 0 \\ \sin\theta & \cos\theta & 0 & 0 \\ 0 & 0 & 1 & 0 \\ 0 & 0 & 0 & 1 \end{vmatrix} \text{ about the } z\text{-axis}$$

$$\begin{vmatrix} \cos\theta & 0 & -\sin\theta & 0 \\ 0 & 1 & 0 & 0 \\ \sin\theta & 0 & \cos\theta & 0 \\ 0 & 0 & 0 & 1 \end{vmatrix} \text{ about the } y\text{-axis}$$

$$\begin{vmatrix} 1 & 0 & 0 & 0 \\ 0 & \cos\theta & -\sin\theta & 0 \\ 0 & \sin\theta & \cos\theta & 0 \\ 0 & 0 & 0 & 0 \end{vmatrix} \text{ about the } x\text{-axis}$$

Scale:

$$\begin{vmatrix} Sx & 0 & 0 & 0 \\ 0 & Sy & 0 & 0 \\ 0 & 0 & Sz & 0 \\ 0 & 0 & 0 & 1 \end{vmatrix}$$

3.4 OTHER FUNCTIONS

There are a number of other functions available with the CAD system that are not directly related to the creation or manipulation of entities, although they do assist the user in working with the entities. They are the various maintenance functions and the inquiry functions

3.4.1 Maintenance Functions

Four functions are used to maintain the usability and integrity of the part file. Two are for cleaning up the graphics displayed, while the other two are for cleaning up the data stored in the file.

Repaint Screen.   When entities are deleted from the part. Their defining data are marked as inaccessible and their graphics are erased from the screen. This erasure is typically accomplished simply by drawing over their graphics in the same color as the background (usually black).

This method can create a problem when entities overlap, however. The overpainting in black appears as small breaks in the other entity that was overlapped. After many deletions in a complex part, the entities begin to look quite fragmented. This can become confusing or misleading unless corrected. Therefore, a repaint screen command is implemented as a fast way to redraw entities on the screen.

The CAD system maintains two data buffers for manipulating the image of what appears on the screen. The display buffer contains image information for all the entities currently in the part, while the screen buffer contains the contents of the screen display only. When an entity is deleted, the information in the display buffer is removed and the portion of the screen buffer showing the entity is painted over in black. The repaint command simply sets all of the screen buffer to black and then quickly recopies the currently visible entities from the display buffer.

Regenerate Graphics.   This command is used when more serious problems have appeared with the graphics, such as missing or incorrect display of entities on the screen. In this case, both the screen buffer and the display buffer are emptied or reset. The entity information is then created afresh in the display buffer from the part file information. A screen buffer is then copied, and the correct display of part entities appears on the screen.

Sort File.   As a part file is used, entity creation, entity deletion, and part packing combine to fragment or mix the information stored within. The sort file command serves to reorder the records of information in the part file into an order that is faster for the system to access. This improves the response time that the system gives the user.

Check File.   Occasionally, information in the part file itself may become corrupt, either through software errors in the file manipulation, or through hardware errors with memory. The check file command provides a method of recovering from these corruptions. The part file is scanned, entity by entity. When corrupt entity information is found, the system will attempt to fix it through the application of sophisticated algorithms. If this attempt is unsuccessful, then all of the entity is deleted from the part, and the user is notified of the problem.

3.4.2 Inquiry Functions

Functions also exist whereby the user can interrogate the system to check certain properties of the part being displayed, either to verify the status and relations of entities or to calculate values.

VERIFICATION FUNCTIONS

Verify Parameters   This command lists the values of all the parameters and attributes of any picked entities. It might be used to verify the radius of a circle, the layer that a line is on, the group status of a figure, or the character font of text that is currently displayed in box font.

Verify Position   This command gives the user the coordinates of any digitized location.

Verify Angle   This returns the angle that a line makes with the horizontal axis.

CALCULATION FUNCTIONS

Calculate Distance   This calculates the minimum distance between any two picked entities, or the distance between any two digitized locations.

Calculate Angle   This command calculates the included angle between any two noncollinear (and for 3D parts, nonskew) lines.

Calculate Length   This determines the arc length of any entity or chain of entities.

Calculate Expression   This gives the user a method of performing mathematical calculations on the CAD terminal. This may be a simple BASIC-like interpreter, or a more desirable pop-up calculator icon that is operated from the numeric pad on the keyboard.

Calculate Area   This command determines the area enclosed by a user-defined closed boundary.

Calculate Volume   This is mentioned now for completeness; it is used in 3D parts only. The user specifies an enclosing 3D surface (or surfaces), from which the system determines the enclosed volume.

There is also a group of functions that allows the user to make inquiries or requests of the operating system supporting the CAD software on the computer. It is a very advanced system that offers more than a few of these functions; some are currently available on research systems only.

Suspend Process   This allows users to temporarily suspend the CAD process and to execute other operating system- level tasks. They can then resume the CAD task and continue working where they left off.

Spawn a Process   This command allows the creation of child processes that run independent of the CAD process. These processes can perform other defined tasks, including another CAD session that runs without a terminal.

Parallel Processing   This is not a command to be executed, but rather a method of executing commands. In this, the speed and power of parallel computer-processing methods are applied to perform the more computationally expensive commands on the CAD system.

Interprocess Communication   When child processes have been created, it is often desirable to be able to pass information between them and the parent CAD process. Interprocess communications refers to a set of functions that realizes this goal.

Consult Expert   As further developments are made in artificial intelligence and expert systems, methods of applying this to CAD/CAM are also being developed. The ability to consult a design expert from within a CAD session and to have that expert guide the user through the design of the part are extremely intriguing possibilities. Work in this area is currently in development.

PROBLEMS

3.1 a) How many different ways are there to define a line? Which of these might actually be convenient to a user?

   b) Repeat for a circle.

3.2 Part figures make actual copies of entities in your part file. Pattern figures do not; they only add a nodal instance to the part file. The individual entities are unpickable. What would be appropriate uses for each type of figure? Consider part size, picking to modify entities, standardization of parts, and system efficiency.

3.3 Some CAD systems have fully associated part figures, producing a "live" database of interconnected parts. Although this is complex and can be confusing, it has one strong advantage. What is that advantage?

3.4 Complex transformations are made from combinations of simple translations, scales, and rotations. In performing the complex transformation, the system does a sequence of simple transformations. Does the ordering of this sequence matter? How might a system derive the order of transformations?

chapter 4

THREE DIMENSIONAL CAD APPLICATION

4.1 OVERVIEW OF 3D CAD

The true power of CAD/CAM as a component modeling and manufacturing system only becomes apparent when used in three dimensions. While 2D CAD is sufficient for simpler tasks, the design of more complex components and systems requires the additional sophistication of a third dimension. Three-dimensional design allows a designer to fully model a part or an assembly in space, rather than merely specifying its orthogonal projections. This is very useful in visualizing compound surfaces and is essential in the design of mechanisms prone to component interference problems. Simple 2D CAD is not sufficient to tackle these types of design problems without the iterative prototyping techniques of traditional design methods. Neither are the so-called 2 1/2 D CAD systems, which are simply 2D systems enhanced with features to allow the easy creation of interrelated orthogonal views. They also lack the three-dimensional visualization power of 3D CAD.

The use of 3D computer-aided design is considerably more demanding of user skills, but the accuracy and precision with which components can be quickly modeled and manipulated are great offsetting benefits. This chapter focuses on the additional tools and capabilities provided to a designer by 3D CAD.

4.2 COORDINATE SYSTEMS

In any three-dimensional CAD part, an essential drawing tool is the ability to work in a variety of coordinate systems. The definition of these coordinate systems must be under the user's control so that they may be defined in the particular orientations most suitable for each part. A set of predefined orthographic coordinate systems can also be very useful, if combined with the additional user-defined coordinate systems. Most CAD/CAM systems have one additional rigidly defined coordinate system used by the computer as a reference system, referred to as the absolute coordinate system.

4.2.1 Absolute Coordinates

The absolute coordinate system is the basic coordinate system used by the CAD/CAM processor in all 3D manipulations of entities. Information supplied by the user in any other coordinates is first converted to absolute coordinates before processing. Most systems use the absolute coordinates as the default coordinate system on retrieval or creation of a part. Should the user define and select another coordinate system for use, the option becomes available of specifying data in the new coordinates, or in the absolute coordinates.

4.2.2 Work Coordinates

Effective use of a 3D CAD system requires the capability of defining and using new coordinate systems based on the part geometry. These work coordinate systems allow the user to create planar entities, such as notes and dimensions on planes other than the xy-plane of the absolute coordinate system. Most systems provide several predefined work coordinate systems with particular relations to the absolute system, as well as methods of defining new systems. One common set of predefined work coordinate systems is: top (which is defined as identical to the absolute system), bottom, front, back, right, left, and isometric (usually the top/front/right combination). All of these systems share a common origin point, and differ only in their orientations, which are arranged in the usual fashion.

The CAD/CAM system also provides a set of functions for creating new work coordinate systems based on the part geometry. These coordinate systems are usually defined at an oblique angle to the predefined choices to give easy access to oblique parts of the model, or with shifted origins to allow data entry in relative coordinate values. Five methods of defining coordinate systems follow.

1. *New Origin* The new system has its axes pointing in the same direction as the current system. Its origin has been displaced by offset values dx, dy, and dz.

2. *Rotation*   The new system has the same origin as the current system, and one axis pointing in the same direction. The other two axes have been rotated about the first axis by a user-defined angle.

3. *Three Points*   The user specifies three points or locations in the current system that are not collinear. The first point serves as the origin for the new system. The *x*-axis of the new system lies along a line joining the first and second points. The third point implies the direction of the *y*-axis. The *z*-axis is defined from the *x* and *y* by a right-handed convention.

4. *Two Lines*   The user picks two intersecting lines. The point of intersection serves as the new origin. The new *x*-axis lies along the first line, while the direction of the *y*-axis is implied by the second line. Again the right-hand convention supplies the *z*-axis.

5. *Point and Plane*   The user selects a point or location and a plane. The plane may be an existing plane or be implied by the plane of a two dimensional entity, such as a circle. The new origin will be at the point of projection of the selected point onto the plane, with the *x*-axis and *y*- axis defined by the principle axes of the plane. The *z*-axis is defined as from the new origin to the originally selected point. The right-hand convention then defines which of the principle plane axes becomes the *x*-axis and which becomes the *y*-axis.

4.3 VIEWS

Views are collections of information describing the position and angle from which the model is viewed, essentially a description of a viewpoint. Many views can be defined in a part and simultaneously displayed on the screen by arranging them in a particular layout. These views are defined, created, manipulated, and deleted by the user as the requirements for viewing the model change.

Four pieces of information are needed to create a new view definition, all of which are supplied by the user. First, a coordinate system must be chosen. In the view, the model will be rotated such that the *xy*-plane of this chosen system will be parallel to the plane of the screen. Second, a layout origin is required. This is a point on the screen that defines the placement of the view. The origin point of the coordinate system selected for this view will be positioned to coincide with this layout origin. Next, a default view scale must be chosen. This will serve as a zoom factor to be applied in the display of the view geometry. With this, the user can define views that appear as scaled details of parts of the model geometry. Finally, view boundaries must be defined. These boundaries delineate the screen area that is available to the view for display. If the combination of view origin and view scale causes a part of the view geometry to fall outside of the boundaries, then that geometry will be clipped to the boundaries.

As mentioned previously, the views are collected into an arrangement called a layout. This layout consists of a list of current views and their layout origin points.

The layout itself has an origin point which is mapped to a particular point on the screen device, a display scale, and a coordinate plane which is almost always parallel to the screen. It is the combined mapping of view origin to layout and layout origin to screen that defines where given view geometry will appear on the screen. In fact, the local pan, zoom, and rotate functions provided on the workstation through valuators manipulate the mapping between the whole layout and the screen. For example, pan works by offsetting the layout origin with respect to the physical coordinates of the screen device.

The Viewing Operation—2D case

In order to convert from a geometric set of entities, and view and layout definitions, to a display on the screen device, a seven-step operation is carried out.

1. The geometric information of the entities is expressed in the absolute coordinate system.
2. These absolute coordinates are mapped to corresponding view coordinates, using the mapping implied by the view definition.
3. This transformed geometry (in view coordinates) is clipped to the view boundaries contained in the view definition. This produces the final view representation of the entities.
4. The resulting entities are then mapped to the layout coordinate system using the layout definition of the view's location in the layout. This produces a representation of the entities in the correct area of the layout.
5. The layout is then mapped to the screen coordinates. This mapping is determined by the current setting of the local pan, zoom, and rotation values. The result is a representation of the entities on the virtual screen.
6. The device driving software that controls the screen device may apply an additional mapping from screen coordinates to the device physical coordinates, if the device has a particularly unique set of coordinates.
7. The device driver also clips the geometry to the physical boundaries of the screen. In this way, entities that have been forced off the screen by the pan, zoom, or rotation settings are not considered for display by the screen device. This final representation of the entities is the version that the user sees on the screen.

The Viewing Operation—3D case

The three-dimensional viewing operation is essentially the same. The only difference is an additional operation that is performed between the first and second steps to produce a two-dimensional representation of the model. The expanded first- step follows:

1 (a) The geometric information of the entities is expressed in the absolute coordinate system.

(b) The entities are projected onto the plane of the view, that is the *xy*-plane of the coordinate system that defines the view. This produces a 2D representation that may eventually be mapped to the screen.

View-dependent Edits

Many CAD/CAM systems provide a facility whereby edits affecting the appearance of entities can be made on a view-specific basis. This means that a particular entity may be displayed with a different line font in different views. A common use of this feature is in displaying lines that would be hidden in an actual part using a dashed font. These lines may also be removed by blanking them completely in the view, a process known as hidden-line removal. Separate portions of individual entities may be changed in this view-dependent fashion, as only portions of them may be hidden behind the part when seen from a particular view.

In some systems the detection and removal of hidden lines are provided automatically by the system by a hidden-line removal command. This process of detecting hidden entities and removing them from display is covered further in Section 4.8 when hidden surfaces and algorithms for their removal are considered.

4.4 DRAWINGS

A drawing is a special type of view, primarily used in plotting. It combines features of views and layouts to allow the user to create a finished product, ready for plotting. Except for two differences, it is essentially a view. The first of these differences is that a drawing can contain other views, just as it can contain geometric entities. This is a feature that it has in common with layouts; it serves as a collection and arrangement of other views, based on a set of drawing coordinates. The second difference is that there are restrictions placed on the types of entities that can be added to the drawing. Usually these restrictions allow only notes, dimensions, and other drafting entities to be added. These entities exist only in the drawing itself; they do not exist in any of the views. This may result in a drawing which contains view-specific drafting entities and view entities only. The geometric entities contained in the various views appear in the drawing, but may not be referenced or manipulated in the drawing; the drawing knows only about its views and its own specific entities.

The arrangement of views in a drawing is treated identically as the arrangement of views in a layout. Each view is added to the drawing with a particular origin in drawing coordinates, a particular scale, and with clipping boundaries. This allows the drawing to show blow-up details of the part in some views, without overlapping other views.

The purpose of drawings is to produce a finished visual representation of the part, suitable for plotting. This plotted version of the drawing can then be used to provide blueprints for non-CAD/CAM shop operations. The CAD/CAM system provides a number of parameters to control the plotting of the drawing:

- The plot may be selected to be of a particular drawing, or only a portion of it defined by a window.
- The user must also define the relations to be used to map between the color and line-density information used on the system, and the color and density features of the plotter. Often, with electrostatic plotters, the plotter supports more line densities than the CAD/CAM system does; the user must select which of the plot densities will be used to show the various line densities.
- A scale other than the default 1:1 plotting scale may be specified to cause the drawing to be either enlarged or reduced on plotting.
- For plotters using a continuous roll of paper, the user may specify whether to plot horizontally across the roll or vertically along the roll. The orientation should be chosen so as to minimize the waste paper from the plotter, although for long narrow drawings, only one orientation may be possible in order to get the entire plot on one sheet.
- For very large plots, the drawing may be plotted as a series of strips that can later be pieced together to form the entire plot. This requirement will depend on the plot size (drawing size and plotting scale) and the maximum width of paper allowed by the plotter. The user must then specify the number of strips that the plot is to be split into and the amount of overlap to be provided for in the strips.
- Finally, some systems allow the user to specify a curve tolerance for plotting. This parameter controls the number of short line segments that will be used to display a curve on the plot. Low values (<20) will plot more quickly but result in circles that do not look smooth or circular. Higher values (>100) yield better appearance at the cost of slower plot productions.

4.5 CREATION OF 3D ENTITIES

Except for the creation of the entities which are unique to the three-dimensional environment, creation of 3D entities differs little from the creation of 2D entities. Coordinate information must be supplied with three coordinate values, x, y, and z. This is the only difference in creating many entities, such as point, lines, and splines.

Some entity types, or entity-creation methods, have an implied planar nature. In this group are circles and arcs, notes and labels, and lines created by parallel or perpendicular methods. In 3D CAD, these entities are created on the xy-plane of the current work coordinate system, or parallel to it; lines created as parallel to existing lines will be displaced in the direction of the *xy*-plane of the current coordinates.

Fillets must also be treated differently in a 3D part. Although fillets can be created that are not parallel to the *xy*-plane, they must lie on the same plane as the entities being filleted. This places a restriction on the entities that may be filleted in a 3D part. The entities to be filleted must lie in the same plane in order for a fillet between them to be constructed in that plane—skew lines cannot be filleted.

The remainder of this chapter focuses on the entities which are unique to a three-dimensional CAD part.

4.6 SURFACES

The implementation of surfaces on CAD/CAM is very similar to that of splines. Where a spline is essentially a linear entity with a shape controlled by a set of points, a surface is essentially a rectangular entity with its shape controlled by a two-dimensional array of points. The spline's *u* parameter is matched by *u* and *v* parameters that vary from (0,0) to (1,1) over the surface. The surface is in its most general case bounded by four splines: $u = 0$ and $u = 1$ as two opposite edges, $v = 0$ and $v = 1$ as the perpendicular edges (see Figure 4.1). In fact, any intersection of the surface parallel to an edge will produce a spline—the surface is an array of *u*-splines and perpendicular

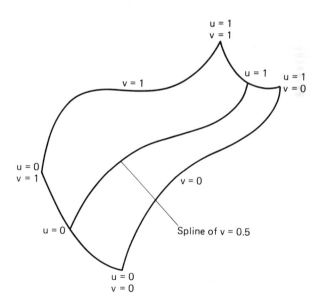

Figure 4.1   Surface *u, v* parameters.

v-splines. Graphically, the surface appears as four bounding splines, possibly with an interior mesh, as shown in Figure 4.2.

The *u* and *v*-splines that make up the surface can be any of the three types covered in Chapter 3, provided they are all of the same type. This means that the CAD system may create Hermite surfaces, Bezier surfaces, or B-surfaces. The particular characteristics of each spline type also appear in the corresponding surfaces. The Bezier surfaces have global blending functions which provide for smooth but difficult to control surfaces, while the B-surfaces have local blending functions which give more control at the expense of less visually appealing shape. Both of these surface types have the convex-hull property, where the volume which is enclosed by the array of defining points is guaranteed to enclose the actual surface. Again, this is useful in aiding the user to visualize how a particular placement of a point will affect the shape of the surface.

Many particular surface shapes are so commonly used that the CAD/CAM system allows them to be created by specifying their unique descriptive parameters, rather than by creating the array of control points. Some of these predefined surface types and their definitions follow and are illustrated in Figure 4.3.

Tabulated Cylinder   This is the surface created when a curve is projected in a straight line. The curve can be of any shape. The common cylinder is a tabulated cylinder based on a circular curve; a flat plane is a tabulated cylinder based on a line. This surface type is created by picking a defining curve, and specifying a direction and distance for projection, either by picking a vector or by digitizing two locations.

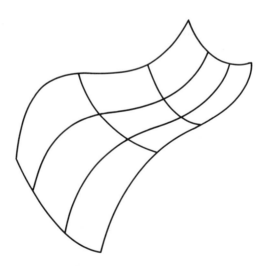

Figure 4.2   Surface mesh display

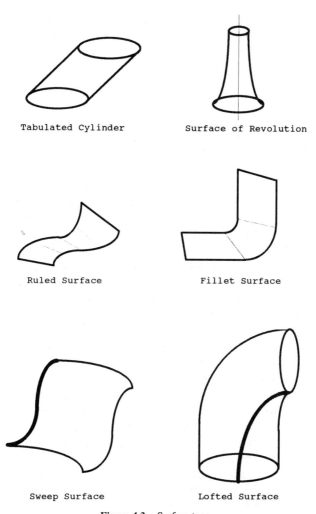

Tabulated Cylinder   Surface of Revolution

Ruled Surface   Fillet Surface

Sweep Surface   Lofted Surface

Figure 4.3   Surface type.

Surface of Revolution   This is the surface created by rotating a curve about an axis. Spheres, ellipsoids, and paraboloids are common examples. It is created by picking a defining curve and an axis, and entering an angle through which the curve should be rotated.

Ruled Surface   This surface is like a general surface where all of the v-splines are straight lines. It is created by simply picking two curves to serve as the $u = 0$ and $u = 1$ edges. Each point on the first curve is mapped by a straight line to the corresponding point on the second curve.

Fillet Surface   This is to surfaces what a fillet is to simple curves. It smoothly blends between two other surfaces. It is created by picking the two surfaces to be filleted, and supplying values for the various parameters required. Some of these parameters control the shape of the cross section (which may vary from a circle to a straight line), or the radius of the fillet (which might vary along the length of the fillet).

Sweep Surface   This is the surface created by sweeping a curve through space along a curved path. It is similar to the tabulated cylinder, except that where the tabulated cylinder was projected in a straight line, the sweep surface follows a curved path. Creation simply requires the picking of a curve to define the cross section of the surface, and a curve to define the path of the sweep.

Bounded Surface   This surface is created by picking four curves to act as the edges of the surface. The interior shape of the surface will be that of a thin skin stretched tightly over the boundary curves. Alternatively, the interior shape may reflect a blending of the shapes of the boundaries, with each edge being assigned a different weight.

Lofted Surface   A lofted surface is similar to a sweep surface but with a more complex description and corresponding appearance. It is based on a guide curve, a cross-section description, and a spine curve. The guide curve directs the surface in space, in much the same manner as with a sweep curve. The cross-section description may simply be a curve or entity, or it may be an entity description that depends on a parameter that varies along the guide curve. A simple case of this would be a circle that changes in radius along the guide curve. The spine curve controls the orientation of the cross-sections along the guide curve. The cross-sections are placed on the guide curve but are oriented to be perpendicular to the spine curve. If the spine is identical to the guide curve, a sweep surface will result, as the cross-section will always be perpendicular to the guide curve. However, the shape of the surface will change as the spine is modified. A circle lofted along a straight-line guide curve with a parallel spine produces a tube. The same circle and guide curve combined with a perpendicular spine curve produces a plane, as the circle is rotated to be perpendicular to the spine as it is swept along the guide curve.

4.7 SOLIDS

Another powerful ability of three-dimensional CAD/CAM systems is the creation of solid models of parts. These models are not just 3D wireframe versions of the part, or surfaced-wireframe models. They actually model the interior properties of the part, as well as its exterior. The resulting model can be used as accurate input to engineering analyses, or sectioned in a variety of ways to create useful technical illustrations of the part.

The solid model is created by the user by a process of building up from a set of primitives. These primitives are three-dimensional objects defined throughout their interiors, as well as on their surfaces. Common primitives supplied by the CAD/CAM system include cubes, spheres, pyramids, and cylinders of various cross sections. These primitives are defined with parametric dimensions; any particular instance of a primitive includes particularly specified values for its dimensions. This allows the user to create primitives of various sizes and proportions.

The primitives are combined to build up the solid model of the part. This combination is effected through the use of logical operators. The constructed part consists of a set of primitive definitions and logical set operators between them. The three fundamental operators are NOT, AND, and OR. These operators act on the primitive solids, and return a different solid volume as their result. The NOT operator acts on a single solid definition and returns all of the volume that is not enclosed by the operand solid. The AND operator takes two operand solids. It returns the solid volume that is enclosed by both operand solids, thus providing the intersection volume. The OR operator returns the volume that is contained in either of the operand solids, or both, thus providing the union volume. Other operators may be considered as combinations of the basic operators. For example, the following two operators can be defined:

$$a \text{ MINUS } b \equiv a \text{ AND (NOT } b)$$

$$a \text{ XOR } b \equiv (a \text{ OR } b) \text{ MINUS } (a \text{ AND } b)$$

The ability to define new operators can provide useful shortcuts in creating complex solid models. In most CAD/CAM systems, this function has not been implemented. However, a predefined set of operators based on useful combinations of the basic operators has been provided.

Some systems also provide for the user definition of primitives. These can be swept solids (see the discussion of swept surfaces in Section 4.6), solids defined as a volume bounded by particular surfaces, or useful combinations of system primitives (such as a shell being defined as a large sphere MINUS a smaller sphere—now requiring two radii parameters). This ability allows the user to create primitives that reflect the nature of his or her application. For example, a mechanical designer may wish to define a bolt primitive to speed construction of solid mechanism models.

4.8 SHADING

Shading is one of the most dramatic features of a CAD/CAM system. The ability to see realistic representations of the three-dimensional part is extremely useful in modeling with surfaces and a necessity in solid modeling. For the designer, the ability to visualize a part in a fully shaded fashion, rather than a simple wireframe representation, can be quite beneficial. This is especially so in the design of parts with free-form surfaces, where the wireframe representation of a surface may not be accurate enough for the designer to make correct decisions concerning its acceptability. A wireframe graphical representation might not highlight a small perturbation in the surface that is sufficient to cause the later NC toolpath functions of the CAD system to fail. Figure 4.4 shows a typical example of the shading capabilities of CAD systems.

The shading capability of CAD systems is derived from a number of models of how light is reflected from real surfaces, and how this can be represented in a computer. When light strikes a surface and is reflected, it may be reflected in a diffuse or specular fashion. Diffuse reflections are caused by rough surfaces, while specular reflections are caused by perfectly smooth surfaces. Real surfaces exhibit a combination of these two behaviors, in a ratio affected by the surface roughness. Diffusely reflected light appears equally bright at any orientation between the surface and the viewer; it is therefore fairly straightforward to determine how a rough surface should appear in a shaded CAD part. For smooth surfaces, or surfaces reflecting light in both fashions, the computation is more complex; the brightness of a specular reflection is highly dependent on the orientation of the surface and the viewer.

With a usable model of surface intensity available, algorithms for the shading of CAD surfaces can be developed. However, before any model can be applied to shading surfaces on a CAD system, a simplifying approximation in the graphical representation of surfaces is required to reduce the complexity of individual surface graphics. This results in a method based on the introduction of surface patches or tessellations. In this method, large convoluted surfaces are divided into a number of smaller relatively planar patches. The shading algorithms are then applied

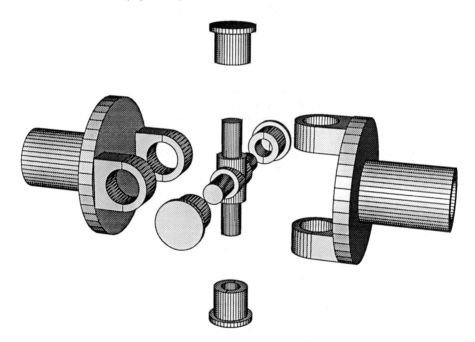

Figure 4.4   Shaded images. Courtesy of Versacad.

individually to these simpler patches, resulting in the overall shading of the whole surface. When the surface is divided into a few patches, the patches, being planar, poorly approximate the actual surface geometry. However, when large numbers of patches are used, much more time is required to produce the fully shaded surface representation. Thus there is a tradeoff between accuracy of surface representation and quality of shaded image. The degree to which a surface is divided into patches, and the resulting quality of the shaded image, should therefore be user-controllable parameters.

PROBLEMS

4.1 Location picks are done using the graphics cursor on the 2D plane of the screen. How can this be mapped into the 3D space of the CAD part? Are there any cases where this mapping might not be possible?

4.2 Fillets cannot be created between lines that are skew (they do not cross, and are on different planes). Why not? What kind of curve is needed to smoothly blend between skew lines?

4.3 Most CAD systems treat surfaces as quasi-rectangular patches with four sides ($u = 0$, $u = 1$, $v = 0$, $v = 1$).

a) How would such a system represent a triangular surface?

b) What problems could arise in manipulating or using this surface?

4.4 A particular line has endpoints that, in work coordinates, are (1,2,-3) and (2,-1,0). The current work coordinate system has an origin at absolute (1,2,1) and is arranged so that its x-axis is parallel to the absolute x-axis, and its y-axis is parallel to the absolute z-axis. The view on the screen is looking down the absolute z-axis towards absolute (0,0,0), with absolute x and y ranging from -10 to 10. The view is scaled on the screen such that it occupies a six-inch square region. How long will the line appear when measured on the face of the screen?

chapter 5

ENHANCED FUNCTIONS OF CAD/CAM

5.1 OVERVIEW OF ENHANCED FUNCTIONS

There are a number of other capabilities of the digital computer that can be applied to the creation of enhanced functionality in a CAD/CAM system. These enhanced functions are developed by taking existing computer applications and uses, and applying that technology to the problems and difficulties of a CAD system. The processing power and number-crunching ability of the computer is used to provide additional capabilities, beyond the basic capabilities of scale drawing and generation of production management and NC information. These additional capabilities fall into two general classes: programming (where user-written programs automate parts of the design process), and analysis (where the number-processing power of the computer provides results from various complex analyses).

5.2 PROGRAMMING

The use of programming languages to enhance the functionality of CAD/CAM systems is a natural extension of traditional computer use to this new area of development. Its use in a CAD/CAM environment entails the same advantages as non-CAD/CAM programming, namely improved speed and accuracy and increased user capabilities. In its simplest application, this programming is used to automate the user's performance of a specific set of repetitive operations on the system. This use of a program to perform these operations immediately results in improved accuracy (as no keying or sequence errors can be made) and speed (as the program executes faster than a user can input commands). In this way, a set of software development tools, tailored to the user application, can be created to effect new and powerful application specific system commands [Valliere 1986].

5.2.1 Macros and Execute Files

The simplest use of programming to enhance the CAD system is in the creation of macros and execute files. Macros are simply recordings of the steps followed by a user to perform a desired action on the system. This recording may simply be in the form of a series of keystrokes on a function keyboard, or menu selections, or the text of commands entered via keyboard. The user then gives a meaningful name to this recorded macro file that allows him or her to later replay it and thereby reexecute those commands.

Execute files are slightly more sophisticated than simple macros. Like macros, they contain sequences of commands to be executed, although these sequences are entered into the file by the direct entry of the user, rather than by recording a sequence of user actions. They may also contain basic input functions to allow the user to enter new parameters for some of the recorded commands, and logical control functions, such as repeat loops or conditional statements.

5.2.2 User Programming Languages

A more powerful and sophisticated approach to enhancing CAD/CAM by the use of programming is through full user programming languages. This entails the use of a fully featured programming language that has the additional ability of performing CAD/CAM functions and manipulating CAD/CAM entities. This fully featured programming language must provide for various program control structures, input and output methods, part and entity creation methods, and part and entity manipulation methods.

This system enhancement by user programming languages can be an extremely powerful tool in tailoring a CAD/CAM system to a particular application, so much so that a CAD/CAM system lacking it should be considered seriously deficient. Because so many productivity enhancing tools can be developed using these languages, it is a shame that many CAD/CAM vendors still offer little or no such capability with their systems. Some systems provide only macro and execute file capabilities. Some provide a limited capability user programming language while also providing full support for a nongraphical third generation computer language, such as Fortran or Pascal. As an example, Auto-Trol has opted to provide a user programming language by developing a set of extensions to existing languages to perform specific CAD/CAM functions, thereby eliminating their need to develop a full proprietary language. This has an advantage for novice programmers in that they do not have to learn an entirely new programming language, merely the extensions added. This does have disadvantages however. Extensions are typically in the form of a set of built-in functions to be called to perform the CAD/CAM tasks. This alternation in the programming style from the linear form of a Fortran-like language to the modular form of a series of function calls makes for programs that are more difficult to write and are choppy and uneven in their form. Also, these function calls are often provided at too low a level in the entity-creation method. In some systems, they do not support the high-level entity-creation methods provided by the standard CAD user interface (such as lines parallel at a distance), but rather require the user program to convert this description into a standard start/end point description of a line. The solution provided by vendors such as Intergraph is a fully featured proprietary user programming language, as well as support for standard third generation programming languages for use in nongraphical tasks. Being complementary to the Auto-Trol approach, it has complementary advantages and disadvantages; the programs are simpler to write and maintain, but they require the user to learn the new programming language.

These types of programming languages are currently the most advanced implementations of user programming languages available on CAD systems. They both effectively implement third generation programming languages. Unfortunately, this level of computer programming has been around since the 1960s. Conventional computer programming has since made enormous strides in power, flexibility, and sophistication. There have been many years of development and subsequent application of more advanced languages/programming systems, such as Planner and Prolog—not to mention the tremendous developments in powerful relational database systems. Unfortunately, the programming environment of CAD systems has not kept pace, it is badly lacking in the power and elegance of current programming technology. CAD system users will require the more sophisticated tools of modern programming methods if they are to fully exploit the capabilities that CAD offers, and if they are to fully realize the potential productivity improvements.

The remainder of this chapter is devoted to exploring the details of the operation of these current-level user programming languages. It covers the various types of statements and functions available in the languages in some detail. It may be skipped by those who wish only a general overview of the subject, or who are not involved in the detailed aspects of CAD system programming.

Control Structures

These statements in the user programming language are used to control the execution of the program. They are common to many other types of programming languages, as this need for execution control is completely independent of the application of the program—non-CAD, nongraphic programs use these control statements as well.

IF THEN ELSE   This is the basic decision-making structure common to the third generation programming languages. The IF part of the structure contains a test statement that evaluates to either TRUE or FALSE, such as (Count = 0). If the test statement is true, then the statements that follow the THEN part of the structure are executed. If the test statement is false, then the statements following the ELSE part of the structure are executed.

```
IF (count = 0) THEN
   some statements to be executed
ELSE
   some other statements;
```

WHILE DO   This is the control structure used to cause the repetitive execution of a series of statements. The WHILE part of the structure contains a logical test, similar to that in an IF statement. If the test statement evaluates true, then the statements enclosed by the WHILE DO are executed once. The test statement is then reevaluated to determine if the enclosed statements should be executed again.

```
WHILE (count < 100) DO
   some statements, possibly modifying count value;
```

CASE   This control structure allows execution to branch to one of many alternatives, based on the value of a selector variable. The value of the selector is determined and compared to the various CASE options. If a match is found, that option is executed. If a match is not found, the default option is executed.

```
CASE count
0:        some statements to be executed,
1,2:      some other statements,
3:        some other statements,
DEFAULT:  some more statements;
```

GOTO   This statement allows execution to be transferred to a different part of the program by the use of identifying labels. Purists in computer programming point out that such a statement is not required in a language, as the same effect can always be achieved through the appropriate use of IF statements, and that the GOTO can be abused so as to create programs that are too complex to read and understand. However, there are places where use of the GOTO provides the simplest and most elegant solution to a programming requirement. However, a well-structured program will keep these cases to a minimum.

```
GOTO Label;
some statements that are skipped
Label: statements that are executed
```

CALL   This control statement passes execution on to a procedure.   A procedure is a self-contained unit of code that performs a useful function.   The procedure is defined only once, but can be used many times by placing CALL statements throughout the main program.   This allows the user to write more compact programs that are also easier to read and maintain.

RETURN   This statement causes a procedure to return execution to the program that CALLed it.   In the main program, this statement causes execution to be returned to the operating system at the point where the user invoked the program.

```
CALL Do_Some_Stuff;
some statements to be executed after the procedure returns
RETURN (to operating system).

PROCEDURE Do_Some_Stuff;
some statements of the procedure
RETURN (to main program);
```

EXECUTE   This statement allows the program to invoke operating system commands, as if the user had entered them from a keyboard.   This allows a program to have access to operating system information, and to perform operating system-level functions for the user.

```
EXECUTE 'List Files';
```

FORK   This control statement causes the creation of a child process.   This new process then begins to execute some named program, independently of the parent process.   This child process many run in parallel with the parent, or the parent process may suspend its own execution until the child process terminates.

```
FORK Big_Program, Continue;
some statements that are run parallel with Big_Program
FORK Important_Program, Wait;
some other statements that are not executed until
   Important_Program is done (but Big_Program can still be running)
```

Input and Output Methods

The next group of statements in a user programming language are statements that allow communication between the user and the program.   These statements print or display information for the user, or request information, either in the form of keyboard input or screen digitizes.

PRINT   This is the statement that provides the program an opportunity to display information for the user.   It can be used to print textual messages or the values of key variables in the program.   The display of the message can be temporary (until the next i/o statement), or permanent (until the next PRINT statement).

```
PRINT TEMP, "The current count is:", count;
```

READ   This is the corresponding statement to the PRINT. It allows the user to enter a value for a variable by typing the value from the keyboard. Both text variables and numeric variables can be given values this way.

```
PRINT TEMP, "Please enter component and size";
READ, comp, size;
```

LOCATE   This statement provides a location-digitizing capability for programs. It supports the range of location modifiers that the location-digitizing function of the interactive CAD system provides. It activates the graphics cursor and gives control to the user. When the user has selected a location, it returns the set of coordinates of the user-digitized point.

```
PRINT TEMP, "Please indicate end location";
LOCATE END, xloc, yloc, zloc;
```

PICK   The PICK statement provides the entity picking and identifying capability of a program. Like the LOCATE statement, this statement activates the graphic cursor and gives control to the user. When the user has picked an entity, it returns the entity that the user indicated. It supports the masking abilities of the interactive CAD system by providing masks for entity type, layer, and so on.

```
PRINT TEMP, "Pick entity to use";
PICK (LINE, ARC), ent2;
```

WRITE   This statement is used to send output into a file. It is similar to the PRINT statement, differing only in that the output is sent to the file rather than the screen, and there is no need for a TEMP or PERM distinction.

```
WRITE ROOT:DEV:USR:DATA, "Count is", count;
```

READF   This is the corresponding statement to read data from a file. It is essentially the same as READ in all other respects.

```
READF ROOT:DEV:SYS:INFO, count, message;
```

Entity Creation

The following group of statements is used to create new entities in the CAD part file. They are a grouping of options and operands based on a three-level hierarchy. At the top are the major words that define what type of entity is to be created, such as POINT or LINE. Next are the minor words that serve to indicate which of the various entity construction techniques is to be used, such as PARAL-

LEL or THREE_POINT. Finally are the modifiers that can be used to indicate location masks, or relative positions, such as END or XLARGE. The minor words and corresponding modifiers are appended to the basic major word as required until a complete definition of the desired entity is created. The creation function then creates the entity in the part and returns it in a program variable. For example,

```
L1 = LINE/FROM 0,0,0 TO 10,2.5,4
```

All entities known to a program are stored in variables so that other statements in the program can make references to them. This storing of entities is essentially the function of the PICK statement mentioned earlier. It stores a previously unknown entity in a variable so that the rest of the program can reference it.

Following are some major words that can be used to create many of the supported entity types in a part, and the minor words and modifiers that can be used with each.

POINT   Creates a point entity. Optional modifiers serve as location masks, and are allowed to be any one of the following:

```
END entity, relative position modifier (to determine which end)
INT entity, entity, optional relative position modifier (for
   multiple intersection cases)
ORIG entity
NEAR entity, approximate coordinates
ATANGL arc entity, angle value
```

LINE   Creates a line entity. Several minor words and modifiers can be used to support the various line-creation methods. Some examples are:

```
FROM coordinates, TO coordinates, (optional HORIZ or VERT minor
   word)
PARALLEL line entity, DIST spacing value, relative position to
   determine which side
TANTO entity, entity
ATANGL angle value, FROM coordinates, LENGTH length value
```

ARC   Creates arcs and circle entities. Some examples of the minor word and modifier combinations supported are:

```
THREE_PT coordinates, coordinates, coordinates, (optional CLOSED
   modifier to select arc or circle)
CENTER coordinates, RADIUS radius value
DIAMETER coordinates, coordinates
```

FILLET   Creates a fillet arc entity. Minor words determine how the fillet radius and center are to be determined, with modifiers to determine whether fillet tangency is to be on the inside or outside of ambiguous curves. Some examples are:

```
RADIUS radius value, entity, optional relative position
    modifier, entity, optional relative position modifier
THREE_ENT entity, optional relative position,
    entity, optional relative position,
    entity, optional relative position
```

CONIC Creates conic entities. There is a selection of minor words to determine the type of conic desired. Each conic type has a group of related modifiers to define the relevant parameter values.

STRING Creates string entities. One minor word to determine whether the string is to be defined by a series of points, or line segments. For example:

```
POINTS location coordinates,…
LINES location coordinates,…
```

GROUP Creates a group entity that contains the indicated entities. There are no minor words or modifiers to this major word. The statement is simply completed by supplying a list of entity variables to be included in the group.

SPLINE Creates splines of the type supported by the CAD system. Minor words and modifiers are available to control spline continuity by determining control point locations or endpoint control vectors. For example:

```
coordinates, coordinates,…
SLOPE angle or vector, coordinates,…, SLOPE angle or vector
```

NOTE Creates a text note entity. Minor words are used to set the various note parameters, such as text justification and character height. Modifiers indicate such things as the note position. For example:

```
coordinates, LEFT, HEIGHT 2.5, FONT Italic, "This is a note"
```

LABEL Creates a label entity. Shares all of the minor words and modifiers of the note major word. Additionally, there are minor words and modifiers to control the placement of the label leader, its origin, and its termination. An example might be:

```
coordinates, LEFT, "This is an entity", LEADER TopLeft,
    coordinates
```

LINDIM Creates linear dimensions. Minor words control whether the dimension is measured HORIZontally, VERTically, or PARALLEL to the minimum distance between the dimensioned locations. There are many combinations of minor words and modifiers to control the vast number of dimension-parameter settings and dimension-definition methods. Some examples of linear dimensions are:

```
HORIZ, coordinates, coordinates, TEXT Auto, APPEND "(Typ)",
    coordinates
VERT, entity END relative position, coordinates, TEXT "2.0 mm",
    coordinates
PARALLEL, coordinates, coordinates, ARROWS Inside, TEXT
    Horizontal, coordinates
```

RADDIM   Creates radius dimensions. Minor words control the various dimension parameters, such as arrow placement, leader origin from the text, and the text format itself.

```
arc entity, ARROWS Inside, TEXT Aligned, APPEND "RAD (2)",
    coordinates
```

ANGDIM   Creates angular dimensions. Modifiers control which ends of the given entities the dimension extends from, and whether the dimensioned angle should be the major or minor angle between the entities. Additional minor words and modifiers control the text and arrow parameters in the same manner as for other dimension types.

```
entity, relative position, entity, relative position, ANGLE
    Minor, TEXT Horizontal, coordinates
```

ORDDIM   Creates ordinate dimensions. Minor words and modifiers control such things as defining a datum, selecting an end of an entity to dimension from, and setting dimensioning parameters. Additional coordinate positions can be specified in the modifier list to control the shape and size of any required dimension line dogleg. Some examples are:

```
DATUM, relative position, entity
entity, relative position, coordinates,...
```

XHATCH   Creates crosshatching of a region. The boundary of the region may be specified as a series of contiguous entities, or as a single group entity containing the boundary entities. Minor words and modifiers control the appearance of the displayed crosshatching graphics, such as in the following:

```
entity,..., STYLE General, ANGLE 45
group entity, STYLE Brass, SPACING 0.1
```

CPFIG Creates a figure, either a part figure or a pattern figure, from the specified entity list or group entity. The new figure is filed under the specified name with a retrieval origin in the same relative position as the specified location. For example:

```
entity,…, coordinates, ROOT:UTL:LIB:MYPATT
```

RPFIG Retrieves a figure into the current part. The retrieval will be by entity addition for part figures and by instantiation for pattern figures. The new entities of a part figure will be unknown to the program since they are not in any program variables. The retrieval will map the pattern origin onto the specified location. Minor words control the group status and layer distribution of part figure entities. For example:

```
ROOT:UTL:LIB:MYPATT, coordinates, UNGROUP, LAYER Originals
TESTPATT, coordinates, LAYER Current
```

CSYS Creates a coordinate system entity that can later be selected as a work coordinate system. Minor words determine which of the many coordinate system specification methods will be used, for example:

```
THREE_PT, coordinates, coordinates, coordinates
ROTATE, coord system, relative position (axis), ANGLE 30
```

SURFACE Creates 3D surfaces. There is a great variety of methods of surface creation in the interactive CAD system interface. In a good user programming language, these are all supported fairly closely with straightforward syntax. Some example specifications are:

```
RULED, entity, entity, MESH 3 By 3
SREV entity, AXIS entity, START 0, END 360
BOUNDED, entity, entity, entity, entity, MESH None
```

Entity Manipulation Functions

The following group of statements are functions which can be used to modify various entity parameters, and thereby manipulate entities. When they appear on the right-hand side of an assignment statement, they return information about a particular entity or entity parameter values. Placed on the left-hand side of an assignment, they can be used to set new parameter values. For example, the FPOINT function can be used to return or set the coordinate values of a given point entity. The following group of statements would cause point P2 to move to the same location as point P1:

```
P1 = POINT/5,10,7
P2 = POINT/20,10,15
FPOINT(P2) = FPOINT(P1) % P(2) moves to 5,10,7
```

Some of the most common of these types of functions are briefly explained here in a generic form. No existing CAD user programming language supports the full set of these functions, with these exact names and properties, although each provides methods of achieving the same general result.

FWCS   Returns the coordinate system entity which is serving as the current work coordinate system. Can be used to set a new work coordinate system based on another coordinate system entity.

FCOL   Returns the current entity-creation color. Can be used to set a new value for entity-creation color by assigning a new color value to the function.

FFONT   Returns the current entity-creation line font. Can be used to set a new creation font in a similar manner as FCOL.

FDENS   Returns the current creation line density value. Can be set to a new value in a similar manner as FCOL.

FWLAY   Returns the layer number which serves as the current work layer. The work layer may be changed by assigning a new value to this function.

FLAYER   Returns a descriptive list of layers identifying which are active, which are reference, and which are inactive. Can be used to change the layer status of various layers.

FPOINT   Returns or sets the coordinate values of a point entity, as previously illustrated.

FSTARTPT   Similar to FPOINT, but acts on the starting endpoint of the given entity (such as a line or arc). Can be used to move the endpoint of a line to a new location.

FENDPT   Similar to FPOINT, but acts on the final endpoint of the given entity (such as a line or arc).

FSTARTANG   Returns the start angle (measured counterclockwise from the positive x-axis) of the given arc or circle. Can be used to set a new starting angle, thus changing the appearance of the arc.

FENDANG   Returns or sets the final angle of the given arc or circle. Similar to FSTARTANG function.

FENTNAME   Returns the name of the given entity, that is the value for its name attribute. This is often used to identify particularly named entities that were created by another source than the currently executing program, such as in a pattern or by a previous program. This function is also used to set the name attribute of an entity to a desired value.

FATTR   A generalization of the FENTNAME function. It returns the value of a specified attribute for a specified entity. It can also be used to set the attribute of the entity.

Text/Dimension Parameters A wide variety of functions exist which can be used to determine or set the values for the various text and dimension parameters of the system. They are far too numerous to list, but some examples may suffice to illustrate their general form.

FDFACTOR = 10   (dimension factor 10)
FDTXTANG = Horiz   (dimension text horizontal)
FTCHARHT = 2.5   (text characters 2.5 mm high)
FDARROWS = Auto   (automatic placement of dimension arrows)

Other Functions

These functions provide analytic measures of entities and their relation to each other, and are often used in mathematical computations to supply key values. Unlike the manipulation functions, they cannot be used on the left-hand side of assignment statements to change entities or their relations.

FDIST Returns the minimum distance between the two given entities, measured as the true 3D distance.

FANG Returns the minor angle between two given entities, typically two intersecting lines. The entities cannot be skew to each other.

FCPOS Returns the coordinates of a location which is a specified fraction of the distance along an entity from its start point to its endpoint. It requires a fraction value between 0 and 1, and an entity as arguments. For surfaces, two fractions must be supplied, one to be applied in the u-direction, and one to be applied in the v-direction, in order to determine the desired point.

Manipulation and Appearance Statements

These statements in the user programming language provide manipulation and appearance modification of entities regardless of their types.   They range from statements that refresh the appearance of the entity on the screen to ones removing the entity from the part.

MATRIX This statement is used to define a transformation. It takes minor words TRANSL, ROTATE, and MIRROR to define which type of transformation matrix is desired, and modifiers to provide the appropriate parameters. For example:

```
M1 = MATRIX/ TRANSL, DX 10;
```

TRANSF This statement applies a transformation matrix to selected entities. It supports a COPY minor word that determines whether the transformation is to move the selected entities, or move copies of the selected entities. For example:

```
TRANSF/ M1, L1;
TRANSF/ M1, GROUP G1, COPY;
```

DELETE   This statement deletes the specified entities from the part. As mentioned in the interactive delete command, entity deletions may be reversed on some CAD systems. DELETE takes no minor words or modifiers.

BLANK/UNBLANK   These two statements cause the selected entities to be blanked or unblanked, respectively. Blanked entities are not visible on the screen, nor can they be selected by the user in an I/O operation. However, they are still accessible to a program through the variables in which they are stored.

REPAINT   This statement causes a repainting of the screen from the contents of the display buffer. It is used in a program whenever the programmer suspects that the screen display might have become degraded through the operation of the program, such as when many entities have been deleted.

REGENERATE   This statement causes the contents of the display buffer to be discarded and regenerated from the part entity descriptions. It is not normally used in a program except in the handling of severe error conditions where the display buffer may have become corrupt.

Part and Database Enquiry Statements

These statements provide the programmer with the facility to inspect part and database parameters in a manner similar to the entity-manipulation functions previously discussed, or to perform file-manipulation functions separate from those provided by the operating system.

RPART   This is the user programming language statement to retrieve a CAD part from disk storage and make it available for modification by a program. It takes as a parameter the filename of the desired part, and optionally its full pathname.

RLAYOUT   This statement retrieves a particular layout (or arrangement of views) for the currently active part and uses it for the screen display. It discards any currently used layout. The layout name is its single parameter.

FILEPART   This statement files the currently active part back to disk storage, overwriting any previous file of the same name. It leaves the current part active on the screen.

EXITPART   This statement causes the currently active part to be discarded from the screen and made unavailable for modification. The combination of a FILEPART followed by an EXITPART is the normal method of terminating work on a CAD part from within a program.

LISTFILE   This statement causes a list of files in a specified directory to be printed on a specified output device. Modifiers determine whether part files, text files, or all files will be listed, and which device the listing will go to. For example:

```
LISTFILE Part, "ROOT:DESIGN:PROJ1", Screen;
LISTFILE All, "ROOT", Printer;
```

It provides a simple front end for the operating system file listing command without invoking the full power of an EXECUTE statement.

LISTENT   This statement produces a dump of selected entities from the currently active part file. The dump includes information such as the defining parameters of the entity, its attributes, and their values. As with the LISTFILE statement, output can be directed to destinations such as the screen, the printer, or a file. For example:

```
LISTENT All, Printer;
LISTENT L1, P1, "ROOT:DEV:MY_ENTS";
```

A sample of the output created by such a statement listing a line entity follows:

```
record length          191
entity index           003
entity type            Line
name                   'LINE1'
layer                  01
discrimination         Red Solid Thin
highlight              No
blank                  No
containing group index 000
attr tag               'component'
attr value             'leading edge'
start                  0.0   0.0    0.0
end                    10.0   0.0   15.0
view dependant data    None
```

Sample Program

This sample program retrieves a user-specified part and adds a note to it.

```
/* Note-adding sample program */
PRINT TEMP, "Enter the part name:";
READ pname;
RPART pname;
RLAYOUT Standard;
PRINT TEMP, "Where would you like the note to appear?";
LOCATE x,y,z;
NOTE x,y,z, LEFT, HEIGHT 4.0, "This is an automatic note.";
FILEPART;
EXITPART;
PRINT TEMP, "Program finished.";
```

5.3 CAE ANALYSIS

In addition to the various programming capabilities that may be added to a CAD system are the advanced analysis packages available. These packages provide tools on the CAD system to enable the user to perform complex engineering analyses with ease. The most frequently seen of these packages are the finite element method analysis packages, the kinematic analysis packages, and the simulation packages. Each of these is looked at in turn.

5.3.1 FEM

The finite element method (FEM) analysis package provides a user with tools and capabilities to easily perform FEM analyses on geometry modeled in a CAD part. The analyses can include such things as stress distributions in loaded parts, deformations of loaded parts, or temperature distributions in thermally-loaded parts.

CAPABILITIES

- The FEM tools allow the decomposition of CAD surfaces into a number of topologically equivalent, planar, and virtual surfaces that are used in the analyses.
- They then provide the automatic generation of connection nodes and element meshes on the virtual surfaces, under the control of user-determined parameters. Sophisticated algorithms for the automatic generation of element meshes have been developed. They allow variation in the types of elements used in the mesh (for example, 4-node or 9-node quadralaterals), as well as in the element sizes used. Commonly, they allow for the use of smaller, more accurate elements in more complex areas of the part under analysis.
- They also provide the mapping of nodes and meshes to the actual surfaces.
- There are unfortunate limitations to current FEM packages that are primarily due to limitations in the available computing power and expected response time. These manifest themselves as an inability to accurately model some types of real-world structures, undesirable dependence on element type, joint type, and boundary condition selection, and insufficiently fine mesh sizes.

LINKS/MESHES

- Element links can be controlled by parameters to provide various material properties: linear/nonlinear, elastic/visco-elastic/plastic, isotropic/aniso-tropic.
- The automatically generated meshes can be controlled in their topology and in their spacing. Some common element forms are trusses, beams, shells, 2D solids, and 3D solids.

APPLICATIONS

- There is a wide range of potential applications of this particular analysis tool. Analyses may include static, transient, modal response, fracture, heat transfer, fluid mechanics, buckling, and postbuckling.
- The most common application is in mechanical component design and analysis. One typical example of such a product is the Supertab FEM system from Structural Dynamics Research Corp.

5.3.2 Kinematics

A kinematic analysis package provides tools for analyzing the motion of complex mechanisms that have been modeled on the CAD system. Displacements, velocities, and accelerations of elements of the model can be easily determined at various points throughout the cycle of motion. Models consist of elements and their properties, connection data to describe their interconnections, and initial condition data such as applied forces and initial positions, velocities, and accelerations.

CAPABILITIES

- The analysis package can decompose CAD models into element descriptions and connection data. These are then converted into a simple mechanism for the actual kinematic analysis. The analysis consists of determining the state of the various elements at certain discrete time intervals following the initial state.

ELEMENTS

- The CAD model is converted into basic elements having three essential properties: a mass, a damping coefficient, and a spring constant.

MECHANISMS

- The analysis of the mechanism is based on the connection data of the CAD model, such as the element geometry, element interconnections, and end constraints at connection points. Basic mechanisms such as pivots, sliders, and cranks are identified and used as the basis for the analysis.

APPLICATIONS

- Kinematic design has its application almost entirely in the area of mechanism design, an area spanning a wide range of engineering activities.

5.3.3 Simulation

One of the most powerful applications of CAD system power, with potentially the widest range of application, is in system simulations. Simulation provides a designer with a method of modeling the three-dimensional configuration of elements in a system and their various coordinated motions. This allows the designer to view the operation of the system and to thereby design improvements to it, without the expense of building or allocating a physical prototype of the system. The modeling of a system can range from highly symbolic representations of flow processes to physically realistic representations of automated assembly line processes.

CAPABILITIES

- The simulation system is capable of modeling the behavior of complex systems, and the interrelationships of their elements over time. This modeling includes graphical displays of the dynamic configuration and status of the system, as well as numerical displays of key system variables.

METHODS

- Typically, the modeling is based on the analytical or numerical solution of the governing differential equations of the system. The numerical solutions are based on derived difference equations, which are applied at regular discrete time intervals.

APPLICATIONS

- There are many potential applications of a simulation package on a CAD system, most of which can be classed together as virtual prototyping. One particular instance of this class of applications receiving much recent attention is in offline robot programming. Here, the simulation capabilities of a CAD system are used to develop and test new programs for assembly robots. The programs are developed on the CAD system so that the physical robots can remain in production use during the development period.
- Another area where simulation capabilities are being put to use is in the modeling of the behavior of electronic systems for circuit design. At Bell-Northern Research, simulation is used extensively in the design of microchips and printed circuit boards for the telecommunications industry [Bell Northern Research 1988].
- Simulation techniques are also used to provide add-on packages for analysis of flow problems. An example is the Geomod package available through the Structural Dynamics Research Corp. Flow-analysis packages typically allow for analyses of complex non-Newtonian flows through geometry specified on the CAD system, such as the flow of plastic resin through a CAD-designed mold. Analyses would include temperature and pressure profiles of the flow.

PROBLEMS

5.1 How can you combine a partially completed part file with entity name attributes, and a data file, with a UPL program to create a system which will automatically complete drawings? (Be specific.) What practical applications might this have?

5.2 FEM analyses yield improved accuracy when finer mesh sizes are used. What practical limits restrict us from arbitrarily small meshes? Assuming unlimited computing power, are there any theoretical limits on how accurately materials can be modeled by meshes?

part two

CAD in Computer-integrated Manufacturing

This section of the book looks at how CAD technology fits into an overall CIM strategy within an organization. It provides information on how the CAD installation in an organization can expand into computer-aided manufacturing applications, and on how CIM can be used to coordinate and manage complex manufacturing systems that include CAD and CAM. Chapter 6 provides a very brief introduction to CIM and the information storage and transmission requirements of its implementation. It also provides an overview of how the many technologies used in CIM, such as CAD, interrelate. Chapter 7 discusses the relationship between CAD and the production planning aspects of CAM. This leads into group technology methods and the use of computer-aided process planning. Chapter 8 examines the numeric control (NC) machining aspects of CAM, and how CAD systems can be used to provide input to the NC machining process. Finally, Chapter 9 explores the communication methods used to link CAD and other technologies together into a CIM system.

chapter 6

———

COMPUTER-INTEGRATED MANUFACTURING INTRODUCTION

6.1 THE NATURE OF COMPUTER-INTEGRATED MANUFACTURING

The ultimate goal in implementing CAD and related technologies in a design and manufacturing operation is the eventual establishment of an overall computer-integrated manufacturing environment. It is important to realize that CIM is not a technology, nor simply a collection of computer-based technologies. CIM is a direction and a philosophy for the management and operation of design and manufacturing facilities. The CIM paradigm is based on the concept of full control over the manufacturing process through a single information source. Full control implies control not only over the direct manufacturing process, but also over the support systems, the business practices, and corporate goals. Thus, CIM affects the operation of the entire organization.

The rationale behind this paradigm is the desire to reduce manufacturing costs in the most effective way. Modern manufacturing methods have progressed to the point where further increases in the efficiency of individual manufacturing operations have become less and less significant in reducing overall costs. Direct production costs now represent only a small portion of overall costs; indirect costs, such as manufacturing support, have become the major contributors. The integration of the various manufacturing processes, through CIM, attempts to bring to indirect costs the same reductions that technology has brought to direct costs [Thomson 1987].

6.2 INFORMATION FLOW AND CIM

The heart of CIM is in the free flow of information, usually based on the electronic transfer of data among various computer systems. This information transfer allows for the effective integration of material-processing and data-processing operations within the organization. This integration brings together the technologies of computer-aided design, computer-aided manufacturing, production planning, and production control through the use of group technology methods and database management facilities.

CIM fundamentally changes the structure of a company by shifting the focus of organization from the function of individual departments, to the information flow through departments and the interdependencies thus highlighted. The effects of CIM implementation can be very wide reaching, touching departments that might superficially seem distant from the new technologies that are being introduced to support CIM. Its implementation therefore requires commitment from the highest levels of management, as its use will reshape the entire organization.

Since CIM has such widespread effects on the structure and operation of a company, it is not surprising that its benefits are equally widespread and often arise in unexpected ways and from unexpected sources. These benefits are mainly found in strategic dimensions, rather than in straight cost reductions. They include reduced labor requirements (both direct and indirect), lower work in progress inventory, and such strategic benefits as reduced lead times, flexible scheduling, improved machine utilization, and improved quality.

A fully implemented CIM approach to manufacturing comprises many activities within the organization and many different technologies. Some of these different activities are:

> *Master Scheduling*—the scheduling of manufacturing activities, such as product runs and quantities, and purchasing of materials, within the company using corporate database information. The schedule produced is used to drive the planning for individual job schedules in the shop.
>
> *Manufacturing Resource Planning*—the planning of manufacturing resource usage based on requirements forecasts and manufacturing capacity constraints.
>
> *Computer-aided Engineering (CAE)*—the use of computers and computer graphics systems to perform engineering analyses of parts designed on a CAD system.
>
> *Computer-aided Design (CAD)*—the use of computer graphics systems to assist in the design of parts for manufacture, and to provide geometric data to manufacturing processes.

Capacity Planning—the planning of shop activities to reflect capacity limitations or excesses in particular manufacturing processes, and to optimize utilization of manufacturing capacity in the shop.

Computer-aided Process Planning (CAPP)—the use of computers and computer graphics systems to plan manufacturing processes and sequences, based on CAD part data and manufacturing data.

Shop Scheduling—the scheduling and routing of production jobs through the various manufacturing processes planned via CAPP.

NC Programming—the creation of NC programs for manufacturing use, based on the geometric CAD part data and the CAPP processing data.

Production Dispatching—the release of raw materials to the manufacturing processes, under the direction of the shop schedules.

Flexible Manufacturing Systems (FMS)—the use of manufacturing automation, utilizing NC manufacturing data, to provide flexibility in parts production and allow more responsive scheduling.

Computer-aided Manufacturing (CAM)—the use of computers to facilitate manufacturing processes, including CAPP, shop scheduling, and NC programming.

Computer-aided Quality Control (CAQC)—the use of computers to monitor the quality of produced parts by comparing collected data with CAD geometric data, and with manufacturing tolerance data.

Inventory Control—the use of computer databases to track inventory levels, warehousing information, dispatches to production, and received stock.

From this list it is apparent the high degree of computerization required to fully integrate these many activities. Figure 6.1 shows the relationships that exist between the major technologies in CIM, and how computers serve in the integration role.

6.3 MODELS OF CIM

There are many models of how CIM should actually be implemented in an organization, and how the various aspects of CIM interrelate. The Computer and Automated Systems Association of the Society of Manufacturing Engineers has developed a model that has become widely known as the CASA CIM Wheel [Snodgrass 1987]. Shown in Figure 6.2, it represents CIM as the four technologies: design and engineering, manufacturing planning, manufacturing systems, and flexible manufacturing. These are integrated through the central use of common data, provided through a database and communications network.

Figure 6.3 shows another model of CIM adapted from Zgorzelski [1986]. This model emphasizes the data storage and transfer aspects of CIM, rather than its

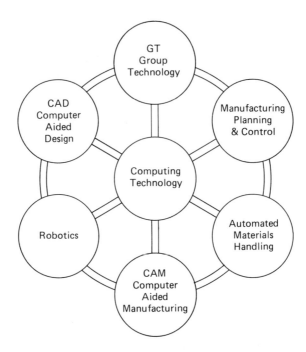

Figure 6.1   CIM technologies.

integration of technologies. This model is based on the three databases: management and production control, design, and manufacturing. The technologies behind CIM are viewed as separate processes running from these databases.

Yet another model of CIM is shown in Figure 6.4. This model is based on the answers to the production questions of what, when, and how. The what and when are jointly determined by manufacturing planning and manufacturing control. The how is determined by manufacturing engineering, acting on the information provided by design engineering. This model focuses on the processes involved in production, and on the information flows between these processes. It does not deal closely with the nature of the information or the methods in which it is stored and transferred.

6.4 DEVELOPING A CIM DATABASE

The CIM paradigm is based on the efficient transfer and exchange of information among the various parts of an organization. This ability is provided through the use of database technology. Without the data organization methods available with computer databases, a practical CIM system could not be implemented. For this reason,

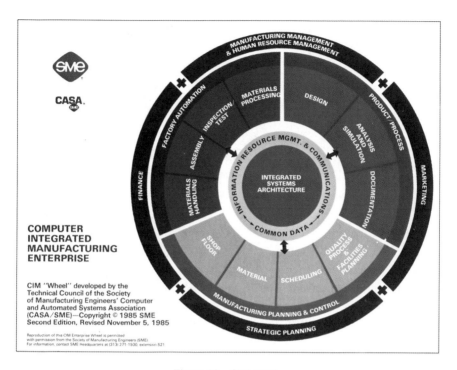

Figure 6.2   CIM wheel.

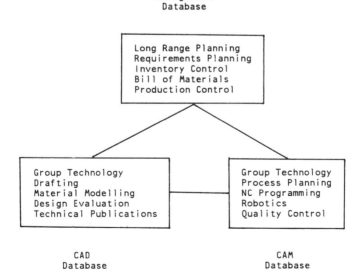

Figure 6.3   Database CIM model. (Reprinted with permission. © 1986 Society of Automotive Engineers Inc.)

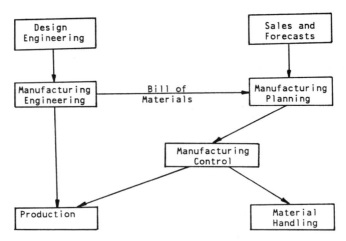

Figure 6.4 Functional CIM model.

it is important to understand how database technology is used in CIM to support its information storage and processing requirements. The information processing is effected by creating a number of related databases on computers for storing and exchanging data. The first step towards implementing CIM in an organization is therefore to establish an initial engineering database. In most organizations starting to implement CIM, the introduction of CAD/CAM technology is thought to be the focal point for the CIM startup. This is the incorrect approach, as it leads to too narrow a viewpoint on the overall implementation strategy. This strategy must begin with consideration of information flow within the organization and with the establishment of an initial engineering database. This database provides for the initial storage and transfer of information between and among existing corporate information sources, and the new technologies being introduced.

This initial engineering database will likely find its major use as a job-tracking tool, as status information from the various stages in the production process can be fed into it. It should be structured to allow queries on component usage data (both per job and across a product line), production facility utilization, scheduling, and individual job status. Care should be taken to insure that accurate data are entered into the database from the affecting processes, or else the database will become inconsistent with the true state of the operation and lose its value.

Developing a structure for the database is a company-specific task. Each organization will have particular information that should be tracked for each job. This particular structure will need to be determined through analysis of the needs of the organization for information access, and by the potential uses and requirements of the database. This also involves making a tradeoff between storing more information in preparation for a future application, and storing less information in reduction of database size and memory costs. One potential structure of the database that may serve as an initial guide for a more company-specific one is the following:

Product Information (name, number)

Bill Of Materials

Where Used (cross reference to other jobs)

Grouping Information (similar to other jobs, or group technology design number)

Drawing Information

Process Planning Information

NC Programming Information

Manufacturing Equipment Information

Tooling Information

Material Information

Job Schedule

Status Information (milestone dates achieved)

Notes

Eventually in the evolution of the CIM environment, this initial engineering database must give way to a full CIM database complement, storing all of the information required by the various processes linked in the CIM network. The requirements placed on this data-storage system will be so varied and complex that it is often implemented via a number of independent databases, linked via information exchange software interfaces. This set of linked databases provides a common source of data to the CIM processes: computer-aided design, manufacturing resource planning, computer-aided process planning, group technology systems, computer-aided manufacturing, and computer-aided quality control.

There are many ways in which these data can be organized and grouped in databases, just as there are many choices in the selection of which data to track and store. These choices depend on the application, the structure of the organization, the nature of the products being produced, and the dynamics of the production process in the organization. One possible method of structuring CIM data is by their application in various stages of the production process. For example, data might be grouped into a design database, a manufacturing database, and a process administration database, as follows.

Design Database   The design database provides the administration of all design data. Specifically, this includes the design files for the products, the bill of material data, and any component data. This information may be further divided into three smaller databases.

• Geometry database (for geometrical part definition)

  CAD models and part files

  CAD drawings and representational data

- Design specifications database (for design limits data)
  Quality measurement data
  Design tolerance data

- Design data database (for bulk design data)
  Material properties
  Component data
  Bills of material
  Group technology classification number (design group)

Manufacturing Database   The manufacturing database provides the information used to control the various manufacturing operations in the plant.   This includes monitoring material movements within the plant, collection process information and status data, and providing short-term detailed shop schedules and orders. It may also be subdivided into smaller databases.

- Manufacturing process database (for CAM data)
  Shop scheduling information
  Process plans
  Machinery required (machine group classification number)
  Tooling required (tool group classification number)
  Material handling data

- Machining database (for individual part manufacturing data)
  NC programs and program execution information
  Tool geometry data
  Speed/feed data

Process Administration Database—This database stores the higher-level management information that ties the manufacturing process to the rest of the corporate activities.   This would include manufacturing standards, material requirement planning, master scheduling of production, and financial and cost data.   This also may be subdivided into smaller databases.

- Administrative database (for overall control data)
  Quality specifications
  Production quality data
  Inventories
  Supplier data
  Job status
  Schedules
  Accounting data

- Materials database (for material usage data)
    Vendor information
    Orders, status
    Material routing data
    Work-in-progress status information

This chapter has given a limited introduction to computer-integrated manufacturing concepts; a full treatment of the subject is beyond the scope of this book. The remainder of this section examines the role of CAD in CAM and in CIM—the processes that it interfaces with and the methods by which it communicates information.

chapter 7

COMPUTER-AIDED MANUFACTURING

7.1 OVERVIEW OF CAM

Computer-aided manufacturing refers to the processes involved in the manufacture of parts and components that can be augmented through the application of computer technology. Broadly, these processes can be grouped into manufacturing planning, manufacturing control, and the actual part production. In each of these categories, computer technology has made advances, both in the ease and in the sophistication with which they can be performed. This chapter examines some of the computer applications made to the manufacturing process in the planning and control of manufacturing functions.

7.2 MANUFACTURING CONTROL

In the area of manufacturing control, computers have been successfully applied to scheduling, as in manufacturing resource planning (MRP), and to the use of group technology methods. MRP is a complex method of computer-based planning and scheduling which encompasses many of the operating aspects of a business, from planning and forecasting to inventory control and purchasing. It is a complex system that is beyond the scope of this book and is not treated further. Group technology, however, is covered to a limited extent in the following section.

Group technology

Group Technology (GT) is an organizational philosophy that aims to collect manufactured parts and components into groups, based on their similarities, to facilitate their production and the effective use of manufacturing resources. This is essentially the forming of groups (or part families) with similar characteristics from a design or manufacturing point of view to reduce the number of unique problems or tasks to be dealt with.

The GT approach yields many benefits in design and manufacturing. It can be applied to group parts of similar design for improved engineering productivity. It can be applied to group parts of similar manufacturing methods for improved process planning productivity. It can also be applied to group parts of similar NC machining resource requirements to improve manufacturing productivity. Specific improvements that can be seen are the reuse of manufacturing feedback and manufacturability information for parts of similar design, less machine downtime for setup changes between parts, and less movement of work in progress between machines and between shops, as manufacturing resources are physically grouped together.

The primary difficulty in implementing group technology is in defining an appropriate classification scheme. The classification scheme must meet several criteria in order to achieve its goal of uniquely identifying each part in an efficient and coherent manner. There are six major criteria for a classification scheme. The first is that the scheme be all inclusive; it must provide classification for all of the different parts being produced. Second, the individual classifications must be mutually exclusive; each part must have an identifier which is unique to that one part type. Third, the scheme must be based on unchanging characteristics of the parts; attributes such as delivery date or customer name should not be used as they will change frequently, causing a reclassification of parts. Fourth, the classification scheme should be based on a consistent viewpoint, either from design, from manufacturing, or from a constant combination of attributes of both. Fifth, the scheme should be user oriented; it should be easy to understand, it should employ user terminology, and it should provide quick identification and retrieval with minimal effort on the part of the user. Finally, it should provide a balanced classification of all parts; each class should contain about ten to thirty parts, with no classes particularly overloaded, and no classes relatively empty [Hyer 1984].

Once an appropriate classification scheme has been designed, it must be converted into a number system so that parts and processes may be assigned their unique numbers and thereby grouped. Two variations of numbering scheme may be used to convert the classification scheme into usable identifying numbers. The first method is the chaining of individual attribute codes into a single multidigit number. This method is sometimes referred to as a polycode or feature code [Hyer

85]. In this system, each digit of an identifying number stands independent of the others in specifying one particular attribute of the coded part or process. It leads to relatively long coding numbers whenever there is a great variety of attributes, since each attribute must be allotted its digit, even if it is not relevant for the part being coded. However, this method results in code numbers that are very straightforward to interpret. An example of this type of coding scheme is the primary code of the numbering method developed by Opitz [1970], shown in Figure 7.1.

The second coding variation is the use of a hierarchical grouping of attributes and their associated codes, sometimes referred to as a monocode. In such a scheme, a particular digit in the code has meaning only in relation to the digits which have preceded it in the code number; a 5 in the second digit would have a different meaning, depending on the value of the first digit. This method can code the particular attributes of parts and processes with much higher information density, using significantly fewer digits than the chaining method, but it comes at the cost of a more complex position-sensitive interpretation of the code number digits. Figure 7.2 shows a simple example of a hierarchical coding scheme, from Crowley [1984]. In practice, hierarchical coding is usually used in combination with chained coding, forming hybrid systems showing attributes of both coding schemes.

7.3 COMPUTER-AIDED PROCESS PLANNING

The primary application of computer technology in manufacturing planning has been in process planning. Process planning is the determination of how a particular part will be manufactured in the shop. It consists of breaking the manufacturing process for the part into small steps, and then determining the optimum method of achieving that manufacturing step. This includes determining the type of manufacturing process to use, as well as the machining parameters for that particular process. It also includes determining a sequence of operations for the individual manufacturing actions that attempts to optimize a combination measure of manufacturing time and cost.

The essence of the process planning task can be reduced to five basic steps. First, the required operations must be determined by examining the design data and employing basic machining data (such as that square parts cannot be made on lathes). This design data would typically be the finished part design file from the CAD system. As part of the realization of the gains of CIM, the CAM processes are designed to start with this CAD design file as their input. This insures a continuity of information flow from design engineering to manufacturing engineering. It also provides an exactly accurate and well-structured form of input to manufacturing with no additional cost to design engineering. It is this well-structured input, and electronic handoff, that allows for the use of computer-aided processes in manufacturing engineering.

Second, the machines required for each operation must be determined. This selection depends on knowledge of machine factors, such as availability, machining rate, size, power, torque, and size limitations.

value	1st Digit part class	2nd Digit external shape	3rd Digit internal shape	4th Digit plane surface	5th Digit holes and gears
0	L/D < .5	no machining	without bore	no machining	none
1	L/D > .5	smooth	through hole	external surface	axial
2		single step	single step	pitched surfaces	indexed axial
3		single thread	single thread	external groove	radial
4		single taper	single taper	external spline	indexed radial
5		double step	double step	external slot	spur teeth
6		double thread	double thread	internal surface	spur teeth with holes
7		double taper	double taper	internal spline	bevel teeth
8		operating thread	operating thread	internal slot	other teeth
9		other	other	other	other

Figure 7.1 Chained group numbering. (Reprinted with permission from Opitz "A Classification System to Describe Workpieces," Copyright 1970. Pergamon Press PLC.)

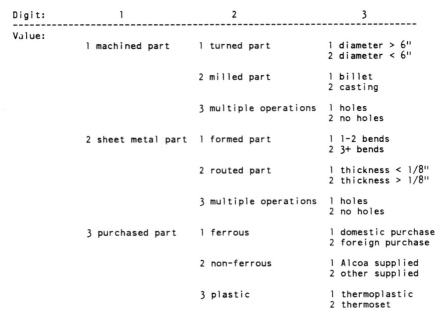

Digit:	1	2	3
Value:			
	1 machined part	1 turned part	1 diameter > 6" 2 diameter < 6"
		2 milled part	1 billet 2 casting
		3 multiple operations	1 holes 2 no holes
	2 sheet metal part	1 formed part	1 1-2 bends 2 3+ bends
		2 routed part	1 thickness < 1/8" 2 thickness > 1/8"
		3 multiple operations	1 holes 2 no holes
	3 purchased part	1 ferrous	1 domestic purchase 2 foreign purchase
		2 non-ferrous	1 Alcoa supplied 2 other supplied
		3 plastic	1 thermoplastic 2 thermoset

Figure 7.2 Hierarchical group numbering (Source: Modern Machine Shop. Reprinted by permission).

Third, the required tools for each identified machine must be determined. This knowledge may be stored in tables of machining data or may be heuristic knowledge of the process planners. For many tools, the tabular approach will suffice. For some tools, this will strictly depend on the process planner's expertise and knowledge of the tools.

Fourth, the optimum cutting parameters for each selected tool must be determined. These parameters include feedrate, cutting speed, depth of cut, and so forth. This determination depends on design data, such as material and surface-finish specifications, and on tool-cutting behavior. As with tool selection, some of this information may be codified, while some will be in heuristic form.

Finally, an optimal combination of these manufacturing processes must be determined. The optimum is the process plan that minimizes some measure of manufacturing time and cost. This provides a detailed plan for the economical manufacture of the part. Figure 7.3 gives a simple example of a process plan for a part to be manufactured. The results of each of these five basic steps can be seen in the final form of the process plan.

Using the computer

Computer-aided process planning (CAPP) involves the use of computers to automate this process. Two fundamentally different approaches to this application have been developed.

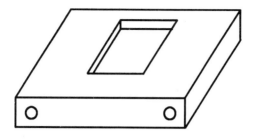

```
MACHINE: Vertical Mill

TOOL-1: 150 dia face mill

Step-1: square to 1000 x 1000 x 400
Step-2: mill to size, tolerance is
        +0.03

TOOL-2: 25 dia four-flute mill

Step-1: mill pocket to 40.0 dp

MACHINE: Gun Drill

TOOL-1: 25 dia drill (850 long)

Step-1: drill to 750 dp (2)
```

Figure 7.3   Process Planning

The first of these is the variant or retrieval method. In this method, the computer makes a search through its store of a number of standard or partially completed process plans that have been previously developed by human planners. Using the current design data supplied by the CAD system, it searches for a plan that was based on a part of similar design. This search can make effective use of group technology design coding to simplify the search for similar code numbers, and hence for similar part designs. This original plan is then modified or completed by the human planner to suit the exact requirements of the current part design. The use of a computer and group technology to search for the most similar past design, and to retrieve the process plan for that design, significantly reduces the work required of the process planners. Their task becomes one of modifying the existing plan to suit the particular dimensions of the current part. They are required to perform the entire process planning method only in the case of a completely new part design.

Two examples of retrieval CAPP systems in use in industry are the Autoplan system of Metcut Research Associates [Beeby 1986], and the MIPLAN system from the Organization for Industrial Research Inc. [Groover 1984]. Both of these systems utilize group technology. The group technology coding methods are used to provide an efficient search of a large computer database of standard and partially completed process plans. Group technology allows the system to search for the most appropriate process plan, according to the criteria defined in the grouping categories. This selected process plan is then provided to the user for further modification and variation.

The second method of computerized process planning is the generative method. In this method, the computer uses stored manufacturing and design data to generate a complete list of all possible process plans that could be used to manufacture the current part. It then exhaustively searches this list for the one which optimizes a specified cost function. This method always yields the optimal process plan for manufacturing a particular part. However, it has a very high cost in time and computer processing expenses. The computations required to produce even a single process plan for an arbitrary part design can be enormously complex. To repeat this for every feasible process plan of a part can become prohibitive.

An example of a generative CAPP system in use in industry is the GENPLAN system of the Lockheed-Georgia Co. GENPLAN creates synthesized process plans based on a description of the part to be manufactured, and on logical and techno-logical restrictions. This description is used to develop a group technology code number for the design and manufacture of the part. Using this code number, GENPLAN may consult a database of machining information to determine an optimal sequence of manufacturing steps for the part [Tulkoff 1984].

Both of these methods of computerized process planning can also be enhanced through the application of artificial intelligence (AI) technologies in the form of expert systems. In the variant method, AI techniques can be applied to perform the modifications to the selected process plan that are currently performed by a human planner. This involves formalizing the process by which the human planner modifies a retrieved process plan. This process is then captured in the expert system. This enables the expert system, in conjunction with the existing search process, to produce finished process plans of equivalent quality to the human finished plans.

In generative CAPP, AI may be used to apply heuristic pruning strategies to reduce the number of candidate process plans that need to be examined. This is accomplished by providing the expert system with rules for detecting trivially nonoptimal sequences of machining operations. One such rule might be to reject process plans that specify repeated boring operations on the same hole, rather than drilling operations followed by a single boring to bring the hole to size. With a sufficient set of such rules, the expert system can direct the generation algorithm to quickly reject process plans that will surely be nonoptimal. This can result in substantial time savings.

PROBLEMS

7.1 Chapter 7 has outlined some classification and coding schemes for parts. Design a classification and coding scheme for a variety of NC machines. Should you use chained or hierarchical coding? Why?

7.2 Generative CAPP can be made more efficient by using artificial intelligence heuristic pruning. What kinds of heuristics could be included to make the search routines faster?

chapter 8

NUMERICAL CONTROL MANUFACTURING

8.1 OVERVIEW OF NC MACHINING

Numerical control (NC) machining refers to the manufacturing techniques whereby machines such as lathes and mills are controlled by a numerical program, rather than by the manual control of an operator. These controlling NC programs may be manually written by an NC programmer, or they may be automatically generated using the capabilities of the CAD system. Many CAD systems provide methods of generating NC programs required to manufacture whatever parts have been designed on the system. This chapter provides an in-depth examination of how NC machines operate, and how a CAD system can be used to generate the NC programs needed to control them. It begins with a look at the machines themselves.

8.2 CNC MACHINES

After the tools of manufacturing planning and manufacturing control have been used to plan and schedule the production of a part, it comes to the actual manufacturing operations required to produce it. In computer-aided manufacturing, these operations are carried out by computerized numerical control (CNC) machines. These are machines that are controlled through numerical-control programs developed on the CAD system. They include lathes, mills (from 2 1/2 axes to 6 axes), presses, flame cutters, laser cutters, and more. The CAD-developed NC programs control the axis motions of these machines, and their operating parameters, to cause them to perform the machining steps required to produce the part as designed on the CAD system.

8.2.1 Controlled Axes

The essence of the numerical control of these machines is in the control over the motion of the various coordinate axes. Physically, this control is provided by fitting the axis with appropriate sensors and effectors. Typically, the control of an axis consists of a control processor which implements the selected control algorithm, a motor to cause machine motion in the controlled axis, and an encoder device fitted to the axis to detect axis motion. The motor may be electric, pneumatic, or hydraulic and may provide linear or angular motion as required by the machine design. The electric motors may be stepper motors or DC servo motors.

The encoder provides information to be fed back to the controller as an error value; this may be the position or the velocity of motion of the axis. There are many types of encoders being used on CNC machines for axis control, all of which serve the common goal of providing reliable, economic, accurate, and repeatable measures of the axis position. While some encoders are linear and are fitted along the axis bed of the machine, the majority are rotary and fitted coaxially with the axis drive motor. This allows them to use a gear ratio to increase the resolution of measurement.

Four types of encoder design are commonly in use. The first is the photoelectric or optical encoder. This device is based on the transmission of light through a thin transparent film on which regularly-spaced black marks have been made. The light is transmitted by an LED and detected by a phototransistor. As the film moves relative to the light source, the black marks successively interrupt the detection of the light. This generates a series of electrical pulses that can be used by the controller to track the axis motion. Figure 8.1 shows how this design can be arranged in a rotary encoder.

A similar method of encoder operation is the use of a toothed metallic sheet in place of the transparent film, and an inductive bridge in place of the LED/phototransistor pair. As the teeth of the sheet are moved past the inductive detector, they individually cause a change in the electrical characteristics of the bridge that can be detected and used by the controller.

A series of regularly-spaced magnets on the moving sheet, combined with Hall generator detection, can also be used as an encoder. This method does not typically provide as fine a resolution as the previous two because of the mechanical limitations on how closely small magnets may be placed, and on the size that magnets may be manufactured.

The fourth method is another optically-based design, called the Multiprismat method. In this design, the light source is reflected from mirrors placed on the

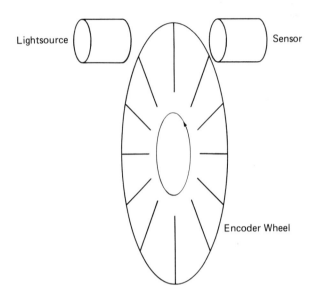

Figure 8.1   Rotary optical encoder.

moving part of the encoder. The reflected light is detected by a series of pho-todetectors, from which the motion of the encoder can be determined. Figure 8.2 shows how the arrangement of two mirrors on the moving part of the encoder can result in a doubling of the effective resolution of the encoder.

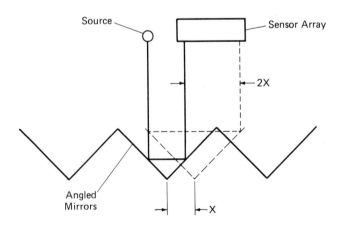

Figure 8.2   Multiprismat encoder.

Many different control algorithms may be employed to ensure the accurate positioning of the axis at its commanded location. All of these use the feedback information of an encoder to provide an estimate of the error state, or difference between the current position and the commanded position. Some provide corrective commands to the motor which are proportional to this difference, or to its time derivative, or to its integral over time. Some provide control which is determined by the motor torque, thereby ensuring a constant force along the axis. Some control the acceleration of the axis. Still others provide control which may also depend on other factors, such as tool wear. Such adaptive control schemes can become very sophisticated. All of these control algorithms are, at varying levels of sophistication and cost, attempting to ensure the accurate positioning of each controlled axis of the CNC machine.

8.2.2 Machine Types

As previously mentioned, NC machines come in a wide variety of designs. Any type of traditional machine that can be adapted to computer control over its axis motions can be configured as an NC machine. Many nontraditional machines have also been designed for NC usage. Some of these machines use such nontraditional machining processes as ultrasonics, abrasive jets, orbital grinding, thermal deburring, chemical milling, electrochemical machining, electron beam cutting, laser cutting, and plasma arc cutting. However, the vast majority are the more traditional machines, such as multiaxis mills, lathes, and electrical discharge machines (EDM).

Often these machines are outfitted with features that provide additional control to the NC programs running on them. These features typically facilitate the use of the machines in high-production environments by providing programmable control over tool changes, pallet or workpiece changes, communication interfaces, and NC program selection and initiation.

8.2.3 Controllers

The controller is the microprocessor-based computer that controls the operation of the CNC machine. It implements the control algorithm for positioning the motion axes, it provides the primary user interface to the machine, and it executes the user-created NC programs that direct the manufacture of parts. Typically, the NC programs are developed on the CAD system and subsequently downloaded into the controller memory, either by paper tape or floppy disk. However, some systems employ distributed numerical control (DNC) where the NC programs remain on a supervisory computer and are electronically transmitted to the machine controllers, as directed by the production schedule and the process plans.

There are three basic operating modes for a machine controller. The first is the normal running of the machine. This running may be as directed by some NC program (either in controller memory or being transmitted DNC), as directed by an operator-keyed program, or under direct hand control of the machine operator as a standard machine tool.

The second operating mode of the controller is to provide useful operator displays on the machine status. These include displays of the machine position and programmed goal position, running conditions, alarms, and other information displays. These are used by the operator to verify correct running of the machine and to prevent damage in the event of severe program errors.

The third operating mode of the controller is to manage and manipulate the stored NC programs. The controller provides a means of downloading programs from the CAD system, of allowing an operator to edit programs, of creating and deleting programs, and of uploading new or modified programs back to the CAD system. In DNC machines, it also provides the ability to drive the machine from program statements received at a communication port rather than from stored programs.

The front panel of the controller provides the operator with controls and displays to facilitate these three operating modes. Figure 8.3 shows the controller panel for a four-axis CNC milling machine. Like most controllers, it provides a large information screen with various displays selectable by the operator. It also provides operator overrides for the programmed feed and speed values. It has a number of function keys for performing machine specific functions, and an alpha-numeric keyboard for use in edit or creation of NC programs in memory.

Figure 8.3   Controller panel.

8.3 PROGRAMS

CNC machines are programmed in a low-level language based on the German standard DIN 66025. This standard treats the programming interface of the controller as if it were composed of a number of alphabetically-named registers, each designed to hold a particular type of information. A line in such a program, called a block, simply consists of a statement of what values should be placed into which registers. The registers, and their use are as follows:

A,B,C—rotation angle about the X,Y,Z axes

D,E—other additional rotations

F—feedrate for axis motions

G—displacement condition

H—miscellaneous functions

I,J,K—interpolation in X,Y,Z directions

L—miscellaneous functions

M—supplemental functions

N—block sequence number

P,Q,R—tertiary motions in X,Y,Z directions

S—spindle speed

T—tool selection

U,V,W—secondary motions in X,Y,Z directions

X,Y,Z—primary motions in X,Y,Z directions

Not all machines will support all of these types of registers; it is somewhat dependent on the machine capabilities. However, the existing capabilities of the machine will be programmed based on a subset of these registers. For example, a single block from a program for a three-axis milling machine might look like

```
N010 G01 X100 Y20.5 Z-10 F30 S200
```

The meanings associated with particular numeric values placed into registers depends on the particular register, and on the manufacturer's design of the controller. An attempt to standardize this has been made by the EIA standard RS-273, although many machine controllers have exceptions to this standard.

8.3.1 G-codes, Displacement Conditions

The G-register and the group of code numbers that is placed into it provide the overall control of the machine motion. They are the most important group of machine programming codes. Particular G-codes determine if the machine will move to commanded coordinates at a rapid rate or at a programmed feedrate, whether the move will be made in a linear fashion or in an interpolated arc, whether the motion should be modified to compensate for changes in tool dimensions, and whether certain subprograms or automatic cycles should be performed on arrival at the new position.

8.3.2 M-codes, Supplemental Functions

The second most important and powerful group of programming codes are the M-codes. These are used to control the aspects of the machine not directly related to the motion of the axes. This includes functions such as the spindle rotation, controlling the flow of coolant to the tool, performing changes of tool or pallet or workpiece, and controlling power clamps or other auxiliary equipment.

Example program

This program is given with minimal explanation so that attention may be focused not on the details of NC programming, but rather on the difficulty of working with a low-level language so far removed from the sophistication of CAD design methods.

```
N01 G71                  absolute coordinates
N02 G90                  metric units
N03 G57 H91              set workpiece origin
N04 T10                  prepare a tool for use
N05 G0 X0 Y0 Z1000       move to tool change position
N06 M6                   change tool
N07 S200                 set spindle speed
N08 M3                   start spindle rotation
N09 G0 X100 Y20          move to start of cutting
N10 M8                   turn on coolant
N11 G0 Z5                approach workpiece
N12 G1 Z-10 F100         cut into workpiece at programmed feedrate
N13 G1 Y60               cut a straight path
N14 G1 Z5                withdraw tool
N15 M9                   stop coolant flow
N16 G0 Z1000 M5          retract tool, stop spindle rotation
N17 M0                   end of program
```

As this example illustrates, traditional NC programming makes little use of modern programming methods and the power of high-level programming languages. It is an archaic approach to machine control that survives only through historical precedent and user complacency. Because of this, CAD interfaces to NC machining have had to ultimately produce programs of this awkward nature. It is hoped that the increased computer sophistication of CAD users will be brought to bear on CNC machine vendors so that manufacturing may benefit from computerization to the same extent that design has.

8.3.3 Higher-level Programming

Some machine vendors have made small steps in this direction in providing higher-level programming features with their machines. This has included the support of user-defined and user-written G-codes, and the support of limited macro statements in NC programs. These macro statements bring NC programming almost to the level of the simplest of traditional computer programming languages, such as BASIC. This is accomplished by supporting statements such as

```
[ SET variable_name = arithmetic_expression ]
[ IF logical_expression, [ statement ] ]
[ GO block_number ]
```

Clearly, even the advanced NC programming languages have a long way to go.

8.4 APT LANGUAGE

The difficulties associated with programming in the low-level language of CNC machine controllers were recognized long before the development of CAD systems. In the 1960s, the Massachusetts Institute of Technology developed a higher-level programming language for U.S. Air Force manufacturing called APT (for automatically programmed tool). The goal of APT was to provide a more sophisticated and powerful method of defining and programming machining tasks, and to buffer the programmer from low-level machine-specific details. Because of its comparably versatile methods of describing geometry and machining operations, APT gained widespread acceptance throughout the manufacturing industry.

APT provided tools for describing part geometry and related machining operations independently of the machine characteristics. This was done through geometric definition statements similar to the ones described in the earlier section on user programming languages. The programs written in the APT language were stored in cutter location source files (CLSF) which were in human readable high-level form. The APT processor converted this source into a binary encoded cutter location (CL) file more suited to processing by computers. The CL files were still independent of the individual characteristics of the ultimate machines to be used. When NC programs were required by particular CNC machines, the APT CL files were passed through postprocessor programs. These postprocessors would interpret the contents of the CL files and produce equivalent NC programs that utilized the specific registers and codes allowed by the machine controller. This meant that a separate postprocessor program existed for each type of machine controller. In some cases, only a single postprocessor program was created, but it relied on many different parameter files which described the individual characteristics of the different types of controllers. Figure 8.4 shows the CLSF for a simple APT program, as well as the NC program that was generated by a particular postprocessor operating on the equivalent CL file. The example shows how the CLSF version of APT provides the programmer with the ability to define geometry and to program machine operations relative to that geometry.

8.5 TOOLPATH ENTITIES IN CAD

The basic CAD entity in NC programming and computer-aided manufacturing is the toolpath. It is an entity in a CAD part file in the same fashion as a line or a point. A toolpath entity, as its name implies, describes a particular motion of an NC cutting tool relative to the CAD geometry. Graphically, it appears in the part file as a complex three-dimensional curve. This curve represents the position of the tip of a cutter following the toolpath. Physically, the toolpath closely resembles a string entity in that it consists of a number of discrete point locations joined by line segments. The complex curvilinear portions of the path are represented by many closely-spaced points and short line segments.

The toolpath provides a CAD designer with the ability to convert the geometric part definitions of the CAD part into machining information that can be processed via the APT processors and postprocessors mentioned previously. Besides having a variety of methods of creating toolpaths (see the next section), the CAD system also provides methods by which toolpaths can be converted into either APT CL source files, or CL files. These files can then be processed using the existing postprocessor technology to produce NC programs for execution on various machines. The nonpositional information for the program, such as tool numbers and cutting parameters, can either be supplied by the designer at the time of conversion, or may be stored as an attribute of the toolpath entity. Some CAD

```
CL Source File                          NC Program
--------------                          ----------

                                        G17
                                        G71
                                        G90
L1 = LINE/0,0,0,100,100,100
SELECTL/7                               T07
                                        G00Z1000
                                        M06
SPINDL/CW,200                           S200M03
GOTO/100,200,300                        G00X100Y200Z300
FEEDRAT/100
GOTO/L1                                 G01Y100Z100F100
GODELTA/-100,0,0
SPiNDL/OFF,LAST                         G01X0M04
FINIS/                                  M02
```

Figure 8.4   CL source file to NC program.

systems store tool information, such as tool numbers, sizes, and cutting parameters, in electronic libraries. The toolpath entity then need only store as an attribute the specific tool used in order to provide all of the information required for the subsequent NC program.

8.5.1 Toolpath Types

It is the particular types of toolpaths supported, and the ease with which they may be created by a designer, that determine the utility of the CAD machining interface. There must be simple, flexible methods of defining toolpaths that will cut the potentially complex curves and surfaces of a CAD part. This section discusses some of the types of toolpaths that can be defined from CAD geometry, and their characteristics. The more complex types of toolpaths apply only to multiaxis milling and cutting machines, while the simpler cases apply equally to simple mills and lathes. The various types of toolpaths are examined in order of increasing complexity and sophistication.

Point to Point   This toolpath consists of a number of straight line motions between points that have been explicitly specified by the user. It is the simplest type of toolpath that may be created. The locations used may be specified by coordinate data, or by location digitizing, or by any of the location specification methods available with the CAD system.

Absolute   The creation of this type of toolpath resembles the writing of an APT source program. The user indicates the geometric entities that the tool is to follow, and the relationship between the tool and the entities (such as ON or LEFT SIDE of the entity). The CAD system then determines the coordinates required to form a toolpath that meets the specified constraints. With curved paths, an under-cutting and overcutting tolerance must be given. As Figure 8.5 shows, this controls

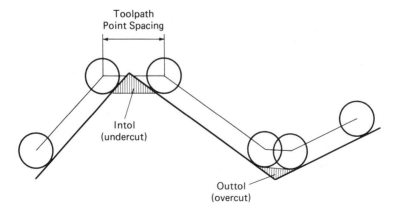

Figure 8.5   Intol/outtol cutting tolerances.

how closely the path must follow the curve and thereby determines the required spacing of the toolpath points in that region.

Profile   This is a higher-level approach to absolute toolpaths. In this case, the user specifies a series of entities that forms a closed boundary, indicating on which side of this boundary the tool cutter should be placed. The system then determines a toolpath such that a cutter following the path would leave behind a profile identical to the shape of the boundary. The user may also choose to have the system calculate side cuts, which are successively-spaced toolpaths that increasingly approach the final toolpath. These side cuts are used to remove large amounts of material before the final cutter pass follows the profile toolpath itself.

Pocket   This toolpath is similar to a profile path in that it follows a boundary, although here the tool is positioned inside the boundary. Also, the system automatically generates side cuts so that the entire enclosed region is cut. The depth of the cut determines whether a through hole or a pocket is formed. In the case of a pocket, the spacing of the side cuts affects the finish of the pocket bottom. This is caused by small ridges or scallops of material being left between the successive passes; closer passes result in smaller ridges and a smoother finish. Figure 8.6 shows a CAD representation of profile and pocket toolpaths, while Figure 8.7 illustrates the effects of side-cut spacing on the height of scallops.

Intersection   This is the first of the truly three-dimensional toolpaths generated from CAD surfaces rather than lines and curves. It is the path of a cutter moving along the intersection of two surfaces. It is not simply the intersection curve, but it is a path calculated so that the cutter always has point tangency with both of the surfaces. This scheme insures that the cutter will not gouge into either of the surfaces, although it also means that the cutter must necessarily leave some material behind in the intersection. It is not possible to machine a perfectly sharp inside corner.

Surface   This is the toolpath used to cut complex three-dimensional surfaces. With this type of toolpath, the designer simply specifies the surface to be cut, the tool to be used,

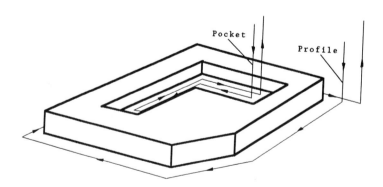

Figure 8.6   Profile and pocket toolpaths.

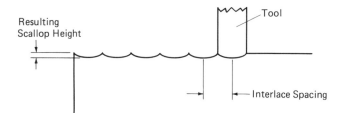

Figure 8.7   Scallop effect.

and the acceptable scallop height (to determine the spacing of passes). The system then calculates a toolpath that results in a cutter producing a copy of the surface in the work material. If the surface contains regions where the radius of curvature is less than the cutting radius of the tool, then the system modifies the path so that no gouging of the surfaces occurs and alerts the designer that the region requires additional cutting with a smaller tool. The portion of the surface which is to be considered for cutting may also be constrained to lie within additional boundaries, such as intersection toolpaths. In this way, one surface may be cut without causing gouging in another neighboring surface. The deep cavities of the part shown in Figure 8.8 were cut by this contained surface toolpath method.

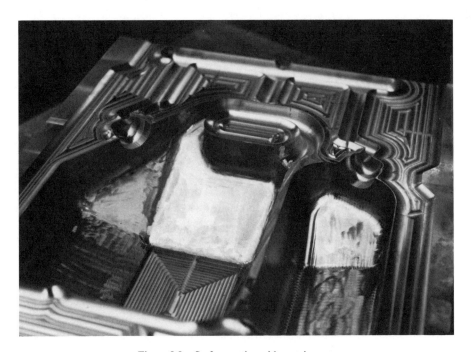

Figure 8.8   Surface cutting with containment.

Swarf   This final toolpath type applies only to those machines having five or more axes or degrees of freedom in their motion.   Where a simpler toolpath describes the successive positions of the machine tool, a swarf cut describes the positions and orientations of the tool.   The swarf cut is made by the side of the tool as the tool follows the path.   Figure 8.9 shows the type of cut that would be made using a swarf toolpath.

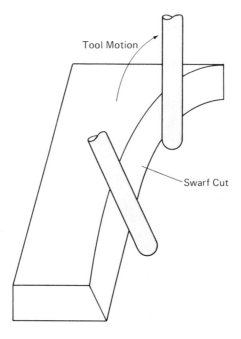

Figure 8.9   Swarf cutting.

8.6 IMPROVING CAM

It should be clear from the previous discussion that the most needed improvements in computer-aided manufacturing are to be made in the machining and NC programming areas.   The current methods are awkward, inefficient, and make little use of available computer technology.   The processes have too much unnecessary complexity with too little standardization.   There are many improvements that can be made to this system.

In NC programming there is a definite need for more powerful and sophisti-cated programming languages.   Archaic programming methods violate all modern rules of software development.   NC programming languages need increased control capabilities and better support for procedural or modular program design.   NC software could then realize some of the benefits long ago realized by most other programming applications.

The program-creation cycle is also much too complex. There are too many steps and too many forms of the same information, existing only for historical reasons. Currently the positional information of the toolpath and the nonpositional information supplied by designer or tool library are combined. This is then fed into the APT process as a cutter location source file or a cutter location file. Then this is postprocessed by one of a number of machine-dependent postprocessor programs. Finally, an NC program is produced which cannot run on a machine even slightly different from the one referenced during postprocessing because the controllers do not adhere to the existing limited standards.

There is no reason for the continued use of APT information forms in the world of CAD/CAM. As a minimum, the CAD/CAM system should store information on machine-dependent restrictions of NC programs and should process toolpaths directly into programs for execution on the machines. The intermediate steps of CLSF and CL file no longer serve a purpose when APT source code is no longer handwritten.

A better solution is to remove the machine dependencies in NC programming languages by the development of appropriate standards. These standards should apply to the form of the programs produced by the CAD/CAM system. It should be the responsibility of machine controller manufacturers to ensure that their controllers can understand programs written to this standard. Obviously, such a standard must be developed with sufficient breadth to cover the wide range of features on different machines, but once developed it would eliminate the need for postprocessors and other forms of machine-dependent information.

Further in the future is the need for applying artificial intelligence technology to more of the manufacturing process. Earlier in this chapter, the application of AI to computer-aided process planning was discussed as an illustration. There are many more such applications for this emerging technology in the field of manufacturing.

PROBLEMS

8.1 An NC machine controller issues a command to move to a location, and the axis servo motor performs the move. Why is a position encoder required? What possible sources of error might prevent the movement to the commanded position?

8.2 The problem with standardizing high-level languages for machine control is the wide variety of options between different machine capabilities. This forces the use of machine-specific postprocessors. What difficulties might there be in developing standards to eliminate the need for postprocessing, both in CAD systems, and in NC machines? Can you conceive of a method of overcoming them?

8.3 A toolpath is being created to cut a surface using a one-inch diameter ball-nosed cutter. The surface is defined as a series of points (x, y, z).

    a) How would you develop a toolpath (set of cutter coordinates) that would cause the cutter to follow tangent to the surface?

    b) How can you insure that your toolpath doesn't gouge the surface to the sides?

chapter 9

COMMUNICATIONS

9.1 LOCAL AREA NETWORKS

Local area networks (LANs) are a fairly recent innovation in the development of computer systems. Basically, they are groups of smaller-sized computers that have been electronically linked together to share information. Each of these computers serves as a node in an interconnected network of computers. Some of the computer nodes act as terminal interfaces; they have terminals of various sorts connected to them that users can use to access the computing power of the network. Some act as server nodes, providing a particular service for all users on the network. Typical services might be operating and managing mass storage devices (tapes or disks) or printers. Some act as communications servers to allow the network to communicate with computer systems that are remotely located. Most devote a large part of their computing power to working on user programs. More complex programs will command the attention of a greater number of nodes. The power of the LAN concept lies in the ability for the overall computing resources to be dynamically allocated and distributed among users, and in the ability for the quick and inexpensive upgrading of the computing power by simply connecting more nodes into the network.

In designing a LAN from separate computers, three factors must be considered: the transmission medium which will connect the nodes, the method that the nodes will use to gain access to the transmission medium, and the topology of the network.

The choice of medium affects both the transmission speed, or bandwidth, of the network and the cost of the network. Cables consisting of twisted pairs of wires offer a simple and inexpensive medium for data transmission. Unfortunately, they also have low bandwidth, and cannot therefore support high-speed transmission. Baseband coaxial, in which voltages or currents transmitted over a coaxial cable correspond directly with the logical bit levels to be transmitted, offer an improvement over the poor bandwidth of twisted pairs, at a small increase in cost. Broadband coax cable, in which logic levels are transmitted as modulations of a carrier wave being continuously transmitted over a heavier broadband cable, is a significant step above baseband, both in performance and in cost. The higher bandwidth of broadband cable, combined with the modulation method of transmission, allow for multiple communication channels to be established over a single cable, each with a high transmission rate. This does not come without drawbacks, however. Broadband cable is physically more difficult to install than baseband. Also, there are restrictions as to where on the cable the various nodes may be tapped in so as to minimize signal echoes on the line. Fiber optic cables offer the ultimate in high bandwidth, high-speed communications, at a tradeoff of very high cost and difficult installation.

Three different access methods are commonly employed in local area networks. The first is the use of polling. In this arrangement, one designated master node successively asks each other node if it has a message to be transmitted to a third node. If so, the sending node is directed to send the message to the master, who then resends it to the third node. This method is only desirable if the nodes in the network can be logically grouped so as to indicate a master to whom most messages would ordinarily be directed. This is not the case in many LANs.

Many LANs use a contention method instead, with all nodes that desire to transmit a message over the medium contending for access to the medium. The most successfully implemented algorithm for this contention is carrier sense multiple access with collision detection (CSMA/CD). In this scheme, the nodes listen to the network line. If the line is found to be idle, all the nodes desiring to send a message transmit their messages. During the transmission the sending nodes continue to listen to the line. If the message is garbled on the line, indicating that a collision between simultaneously transmitted messages has occurred, each sending node waits for a random period of time and then tries to resend its message. Obviously, this contention method can be wasteful of the line's capacity, as potentially large blocks of time are lost due to collisions and random waits. Also, the access time for any given node is indeterminate, and can approach infinity, effectively removing the node from the network. Finally, the response of the network to the sending desire of any node can drop dramatically as the traffic on the network is increased, as more and more time is wasted in collisions.

Another method of controlling access to the medium, without the potential waste of contention, is through a token-passing scheme. In this arrangement, a particularly structured message, called the token, is circulated around the network. When a node desires to send a message, it must wait until it comes into possession of the token. When the token arrives at the node, it is removed from the network. The message is then transmitted by the node, and the token is returned to the network. This insures that no messages will collide with another and be destroyed. It also allows the network designer to prioritize nodes; if some nodes are permitted to send multiple messages before relinquishing the token, their tasks will receive a better overall response from the network. The main difficulty encountered with token-passing schemes is that the frequent manipulation of the token message often results in it becoming degraded or unrecognizable. One node on the network must therefore have the task of monitoring the state of the token. If the token becomes degraded, it must be destroyed and a new token generated and sent onto the network.

The topology of the network is the third factor to be considered in the design of a LAN. Figure 9.1 shows the layout of four common network topologies. The star configuration is desirable for cases where the majority of messages will be to or from one particular node, such as when using a polling-access scheme. An example might be a LAN with a single file server node (hard disk) and multiple terminal servers supporting many users of the same files. The true network configuration offers

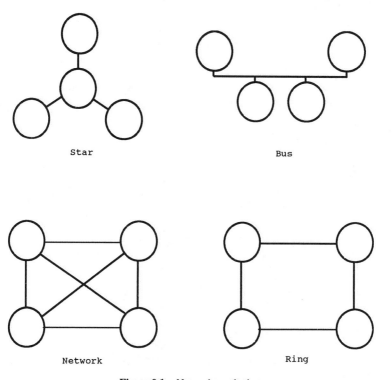

Star

Bus

Network

Ring

Figure 9.1   Network topologies.

the shortest routing between any two nodes, as all nodes are directly connected. However, it is wasteful of communication channels and ports on the nodes and should not be used unless the distances between nodes are large enough to warrant direct interconnection. The bus configuration consists of a single cable backbone into which servers are tapped. It is one of the most popular arrangements for LANs. The ring configuration is closely related to the bus; servers are tapped into a backbone cable which is now in the form of a closed ring. Messaging over the ring is accomplished by dividing the ring into a number of buffers that circulate around the ring. In some cases, the number of buffers is fixed, and a node that wishes to transmit must wait for an empty buffer and then fill it with the message and address it to another node. The receiving node then copies the message out of the buffer and marks it as empty. In other cases, the number of buffers in the ring may vary, and a node transmits by inserting its message directly into the buffer stream that is circulating. The receiving node then removes the message from the buffer stream.

Many standards for LAN design have been proposed, both by standards organizations and by vendors. More are being created as the technology continues to advance. Currently, the most widely accepted standards are:

- Ethernet (IEEE 802.3):
    medium—baseband coaxial cable
    access method—CSMA/CD
    topology—bus configuration
    transmission speed—10Mbps
- Manufacturing Automation Protocol (MAP) (IEEE 802.4):
    medium—broadband coaxial cable
    access method—token passing
    topology—bus configuration
    transmission speed—5 or 10 Mbps
- IBM Token Ring (IEEE 802.5):
    medium—twisted pair
    access method—token passing
    topology—ring configuration
    transmission speed—1 or 4 Mbps
- IEEE 802.6 Fiber Optics:
    metropolitan area network
    high-speed network design, under development.
- PBX-based LANs:
    medium—telephone cable and PBX switch
    access method—PBX call processing methods
    topology—switched network (hybrid between star and true network)
    transmission speed—varies with PBX technology

ISO model - open systems interconnect

There has been an increasing awareness in the computer industry of the importance of the communications compatibility of systems to the overall achievement of user goals. This has manifested itself as a move toward an open environment and architecture in computer systems that allows different systems to communicate freely. This has required the development of various communication standards for these open systems. The international standards organization ISO has defined a standard for describing communication networks based on a seven-layer model. Each layer is defined to perform certain functions for the next higher layer, without regard to the inner workings of the lower layers that it uses. The seven layers are:

Layer 1: Physical (hardware).   This layer deals with the lowest level of communication, the physical connections and hardware definitions. It defines the representation of logical bits by giving a definition of 0 or 1 (by voltage levels, and so on), the physical cable and connector types, and the pin assignments in the connector. It also specifies if the connection is to be simplex (in which the data flow in one direction only), half duplex (in which data can flow in either direction, but not simultaneously), or full duplex (in which data can flow in both directions simultaneously). All mechanical, electrical, or basic procedural considerations are dealt with at this layer.

Layer 2: Link (node addressing).   The goal of this layer is to make the communication path established in Layer 1 look error free to the higher levels. It has the responsibility for recognizing and recovering from transmission errors. The software of Layer 2 breaks data packets into frames to be transmitted, and reassembles the packets on reception. These frames may be either data frames or acknowledge frames sent for control purposes. These frames are actually called "data-link-service-units" by ISO, a descriptive if somewhat unwieldy name. Through the transmission of data frames and the receipt of acknowledge frames, Layer 2 detects damaged or lost frames and retransmits them. It also deals with the more complex cases such as combined errors in both transmission paths.

Layer 3: Network (hides structure).   This layer is responsible for making the network appear as a homogeneous whole, despite the variety of configurations that it might exhibit. It hides topology, gateways, media, and such from the higher layers. It is at this level that data records are disassembled into individual packets for transmitting. The Packet Assembler/Disassembler reconstructs data from received packets. The network level also decides the details of the routing of packets through the network, and tracks accounting and billing information, since this is usually dependent on the routing.

Layer 4: Transport (packet switching).   This layer of the system manages the network and isolates the host computer from all of the hardware aspects of the network. The transport layer may direct the software of Layer 3 to switch packets via several equivalent routes to effect a high single high-speed route. This layer also supports user service levels, such as guaranteed error-free point to point, general broadcast, or one-shot messages.

Layer 5: Session (user connection). This is the first layer of the model that is high enough for the user to have direct access to. It establishes the connection between the user and the desired host system on the network through a process known as binding. It is responsible for initiating the log-on process and for the logical attaching of devices.

Layer 6: Presentation (functions). This layer provides functions that control the way in which the session is presented to the user. It controls the selection of character sets to be used and provides libraries of commonly used functions, such as text compression and character set conversions.

Layer 7: Application (user program). It is at this layer in the model that actual user application programs run. The inner workings and structure of the network are completely transparent and of no consequence to the application program. This standard reference model and the IEEE standard network configurations have been eagerly awaited by many vendors who felt that assured interconnectivity with their competitors' systems was in their best long-term interests. The standard protocols have been widely embraced in the industry. As early as 1985, large-scale demonstrations of complex networks made of interconnected systems from many vendors were being given. Figure 9.2 shows a complex network, demonstrated at Autofact '85, that successfully interconnected many different computer systems.

The operation of the network

As previously mentioned, the LAN consists of a variety of computing nodes that are interconnected by a network. Some nodes act as terminal servers, providing

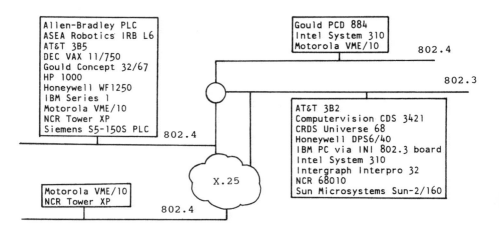

Figure 9.2   MAP network.

user access to the services of the LAN. These nodes may contain processors, memory, or even mass storage devices depending on the complexity and require-ments of the terminal device. Other nodes act as servers, providing network access to resources that must be shared among users. These include file servers that manage disk storage of files, tape servers that manage tape drives, and communi-cation servers that manage communication ports to outside the LAN. Some nodes serve maintenance functions, such as token regeneration, or the elimination of bad packets of data that have not been received by their destination nodes. A fourth type of node is the gateway node. This node allows various LANs using various media, access methods, and topologies to be connected as a single larger LAN. The gateway node manages the conversion between the two protocols, thus allowing nodes on one LAN to send messages to nodes on the other LAN as if they were in the same immediate network. In this way, the gateway acts more like a construction element of the network, like cable taps or head-end remodulators, rather than a user accessible server node.

The operating system differs considerably from the operating systems of single processor computer systems. It must contend with the complexities of distributing the processing load among the computing nodes, allocating working storage provided by nodes, and the increased complexity of directory structures with multiple root nodes on different file servers. One particular node on the network may serve as the operation processor, continuously monitoring the network status, and providing a "network operator" user with information about line contention or traffic levels.

9.2 INTERSYSTEM COMMUNICATION TRANSLATING

As the use of computers in engineering and manufacturing becomes more widespread, there is an increasing demand for facilities by which many different computer systems can communicate with each other. In CAD applications, this problem is compounded by the fact that CAD systems created by different vendors often have widely varying characteristics: they store and manipulate entity information in different ways, and may in fact use somewhat different entity types in their parts. To solve this problem and make it possible to communicate CAD parts from one system to another vendor's system, translator programs were developed. As the number of CAD vendors grew, however, the number of intersystem translators required grew exponentially. Thus, a need for a single neutral format was realized. This neutral format stores CAD information that is used solely by no particular CAD vendor. However, individual vendors now need only provide translators to preprocess their part data from their own format into the neutral format, and postprocess data from the neutral format back again. Converting from System A to System B no longer requires the development of a special A to B translator. The CAD part is simply translated from System A into the neutral format, and from there is translated into System B. If a new type of system is developed by another vendor, that vendor need only create a neutral format translator to immediately enable communications and file transfers with all other types of CAD systems. Figure 9.3 shows how the use of this neutral format greatly reduces the number of translators required in a hypothetical world of six different system types.

In developing a neutral format, it must be determined exactly what data types the format will have to support. For a CAD/CAM neutral file format, it is desirable to have the neutral format support all of the product definition data. This includes the geometry of the part, the administrative data (such as process planning information), any analysis data, material properties, material treatment and processing information, and presentational data (such as notes and captions). The development of this ideal neutral format for CAD/CAM is still taking place. Currently, the most widely used is the Initial Graphics Exchange Specification (IGES). IGES, while still evolving, is committed to upwards compatibility so that future versions of IGES translators will still be able to manipulate parts now saved in the current IGES

Without Neutral Format

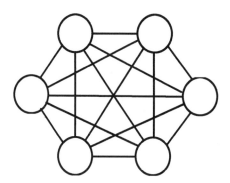

6 Systems = 15 Translators

With Neutral Format

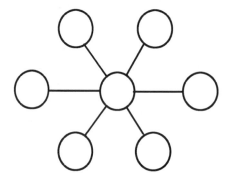

6 Systems = 6 Translators

Figure 9.3   Reduction of interconnections by neutral formats.

format. The development of IGES and other neutral formats is the subject of the next section.

9.2.1 Neutral Formats

General requirements of an interface

There are a number of requirements that should be met by a file-based interface for it to serve effectively as a neutral format. The goal of these requirements is to provide a standard that is clearly specified, and that provides an unambiguous and nonredundant way of describing CAD/CAM information.

The interface must be based on a published formal description. This allows vendors to develop pre- and postprocessing translators for their systems that can be assured to meet the standard. The need for a formal statement of the standard is self-evident, and is well provided by all currently popular neutral format specifications.

The file structure chosen should be efficient. There should be a good balance between the conflicting objectives of a well-packed file with a high-information density, and a file that is easy to access by many different types of computer systems.

There should be a clear classification of the different entity types. This enables the vendor to easily determine which of the supported neutral entities will most closely match his or her own entity types. The entities supported and classified should also be nonredundant, in that there should be no overlap in their representational powers; it should not be possible to represent a vendor's entity by more than one of the neutral format entity types. This helps to prevent uncertainties in the translations of various vendor entity types.

Finally, the conversion algorithms used between the two entity representation methods must be correct and unambiguous. This is an obvious necessity if the transfer of the CAD/CAM information through the neutral file process is to remain faithful to the original design information.

Historical development of neutral formats

The development of appropriate neutral file formats and translators has been progressing steadily throughout the 1980s, with systems becoming more sophisticated in their ability to deal with more complex CAD/CAM information and entity types. Following are some of the highlights of this development.

- Early work was begun by Boeing in its creation of a CAD/CAM integrated information network (CIIN) and by General Electric's development of a neutral database (NDB) format. These early neutral formats were released to industry through the National Bureau of Standards (NBS) in the United States.
- This first neutral format information was then codified by the American National Standards Institute (ANSI) as the standard specification ANSI Y14.26M in 1981.

- Later that year, the NBS created a working group mandated to develop a neutral file format for industrial use. Their recommendation was called the Initial Graphics Exchange Specification (IGES), based on Sections 2 through 4 of the ANSI Y14.26M standard. Section 5 of that standard, which deals with surfaces and solids in a highly efficient manner, was omitted because it was felt that the underlying mathematics would be too difficult to implement [Wiessflog 1986].

- In 1982 Version 2.0 of IGES was released. This version provided additional support of general surfaces, printed circuit board design entities, and finite element methods entities. Also, an optional binary file structure was defined. This was provided in answer to complaints that the initial IGES file structure was too inefficient in its use of space, resulting in IGES format files that were several times larger than the original CAD files. This binary format was not, however, widely implemented by CAD/CAM vendors.

- Work also progressed in Europe during this time. The German industrial societies Verband der Automobilindustrie (VDA) and Verband Deutscher Maschinen-und Anlagenbau e.V. (VDMA) had developed a neutral format called VDAFS that was standardized by DIN in 1983. The VDAFS system has been successful in the automotive industry, but not elsewhere, due to its powerful surfacing capabilities but limited entity set. Its entity set is limited to points, point sequences, point/vector (machining) sequences, piecewise polynomial curves, and piecewise polynomial surfaces [Renz 1986].

- Version 3.0 of IGES appeared in 1986 with modifications to support more surfaces, plant design entities, architectural entities, and more electrical and FEM applications.

Future developments in neutral formats

- At the time of writing, Version 4.0 of IGES is due to be available. The major enhancement to be made over the previous version is the added support of solid modeling entities.

- A version of VDAFS that supports nonrectangular surfaces and topological data is under development.

- A true neutral exchange of complete product definition data is being developed by the U.S. Air Force. Called the Product Definition Data Interface (PDDI), this system will be capable of exchanging the full set of PD data between various CAD/CAM systems, rather than just the geometric information.

- A similar PD data exchange format is also being developed by the IGES community. This Product Data Exchange Standard (PDES) will be based on high-level primitives such as solids, holes, flanges, and ribs. The manufacturing tolerances will be specified by envelopes of acceptable range, rather than by tolerances. Like the PDDI system, it will also incorporate the nongeometric PD data. This system is planned to have an approximate release date of 1990.

Proprietary exchange formats

Several CAD/CAM vendors and developers have also developed formats for CAD/CAM information that they have tried to promote for use as neutral formats. This has met with limited success, as vendors would only develop translators for another's format under considerable pressure from the user community. Some of these formats are listed.

- Intergraph has developed a Standard Interchange Format (SIF) that is also being supported by Applicon, Autotrol, and Calma. This format is used primarily for mapping, petrophysical exploration, and facilities management applications.

- Vought Corporation's Standard product Data exchange file Format (SDF) is being used in aerospace applications. It is also being supported by CADAM, PATRAN, and Computervision.

- The Ford Motor Company has defined a Ford Standard format for communicating automotive design application data with suppliers. This is also supported by some CAD vendors.

- Aerospatiale has defined a Standard D'Exchange et de Transfer (SET) neutral format. This format is considerably more compact than IGES due to the SET use of a block concept similar to patterns.

9.2.2 IGES Structure

In North America, the IGES neutral format is by far the format of choice and promises to remain so for some time to come. It is therefore worthwhile to take a somewhat closer look at how the IGES system works.

IGES entity set

One possible reason for the popularity of IGES is the wide spectrum of entity types that it supports. Most vendors find that almost all of their entities can be successfully represented by an IGES entity. On the other hand, the list of entities is so large that a certain amount of overlap occurs between some entity types. This can cause some entities to pass from one vendor's system to another's and end up represented in the final system by an entity type that is not the best choice. The following list gives some of the IGES entity types with subtypes for some cases. The entities marked with * are not defined by IGES, and are therefore open to interpretation by vendors.

100 circular arc
102 composite curve

104 general conic
106 (1–3) copious data, coordinates
106 (7) vector *
106 (8) point set *
106 (10) machine curve *
106 (11) string *
106 (12–13) linear curve
106 (20) centerline
106 (21) circle centerline
106 (31) crosshatching
106 (32–38) section
106 (40) witness line
106 (63) simple closed area
108 plane
110 line
112 (3) cubic spline 2D
112 (4) Wilson Fouler spline 3D
112 (6) b-spline
114 parametric spline surface
116 point
118 ruled surface
120 surface of revolution
122 tabulated cylinder
124 transformation matrix
125 flash
126 rational b-spline
128 rational b-spline surface
134 node
136 finite element
202 angular dimension
206 diameter dimension
208 flag note
210 general label
212 general note
214 leader, arrow
216 linear dimension
218 ordinate dimension

220 point dimension

222 radius dimension

302 associativity definition

304 line font definition

306 macro definition

308 subfigure definition

310 text font definition

402 (1) associativity instance, group

402 (3) visible view

402 (5) entity name

402 (6) view list

402 (10) text node

404 drawing

406 property

408 subfigure instance

410 view

412 rectangular array

414 circular array

600–699 macro

IGES file structure

The IGES file itself consists of five different sections. The first is the start section. This contains text in a human-readable form that serves to identify the part, the sending and receiving organizations and CAD/CAM systems, revision information, and so forth.

The second section is the global section. This section contains information and directives for the postprocessor that will read the file. This information includes the choice of delimiter character used, the precision used for real numbers, the measurement units used, and the name of the CAD part file from which the IGES file was created. The directory entry section follows the global section. It consists of two fixed format records for each entity described in the file. These records contain entity-independent information such as attribute data, view information, transformation matrices to locate the entity from the origin, and a pointer to one or more records in the next section of the file.

The next section is the parameter data section. As its name implies, this section contains all of the parametric and entity-dependent information for the individual entities in one or more records. These records have different formats for each of the different entity types supported by IGES.

Finally, there is a terminate section. This consists of a single record that gives the byte counts for each of the previous sections.

The vast majority of the information in the IGES file is contained in the directory entry and parameter data sections. The uncompressed nature of these sections accounts for the large size of IGES format files. As mentioned previously, an IGES file may be many times larger than the original CAD file from which it was created.

9.2.3 Problems with Neutral Formats

The creation of neutral file formats is still under development. There exist problems with neutral formats as a group, and with IGES in particular. One significant problem is with the lack of commonality of entity sets. In translating CAD/CAM information, some entity types will not be supported by either the receiving CAD/CAM system or the neutral format, or will be only partially supported via a conversion. This lack of conversion, or misconversion, obviously leads to loss of information during the translation from one system to another. Figure 9.4 shows how this information loss can occur.

As mentioned previously, there is also an unresolved problem with the actual structure of the neutral format file. The conflicting requirements of an efficient, packed structure for fast processing and a highly structured inefficient file for ease of access by many systems are difficult to balance in an optimal combination.

Finally, there are problems with achieving full vendor support of the neutral format. The full entity set and structural options might not be supported by a particular vendor. Vendors typically do not support unusual entity types, especially if there is no direct counterpart in their own systems. The advantage gained may not seem to justify the additional development effort for the translator. This leaves the users somewhat uncertain as to the extent to which the neutral format is

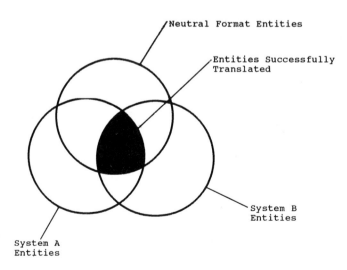

Figure 9.4   Information loss in translations.

supported by their system. This is especially a problem with IGES, as the NBS, who is the organization behind IGES, has not been mandated by the U.S. government to certify vendor versions of the IGES format.

9.3 OTHER COMMUNICATIONS

Two other communications systems deserve to be examined in conjunction with CAD/CAM. The first is the system by which individual devices in a workstation or manufacturing cell communicate among themselves. This interdevice communication has long been dominated by various serial data transfer methods, each with its own particular merits.

The second system to be examined is the expansion of the local area network concept into larger networks that span several computing sites. These wide area networks can link CAD design offices in one city to one or more CAM shops in distant cities, and can link separate LANs into a single virtual LAN that spans several offices in different locations.

9.3.1 Interdevice Serial Communication

The majority of interdevice communications, such as might occur between an NC machine controller and a DNC computer, is accomplished by serial data transfer. In serial communications, the individual bits that make up the data bytes are sent sequentially down a pair of conductors to the receiving device. That device then reconstructs the data bytes from its incoming bit stream. Additional bits are also transmitted using a specific protocol to aid in error detection and prevention. This includes bits to indicate the start of a character, the end of a character, and parity checking bits. There are often other conductors in the communication cable that serve other protocol functions, such as flow control or signaling.

In North America, standards for serial communication protocols are set by the Electronic Industries Association (EIA). These standards can be identified by their RS-prefix. Internationally, the International Telephonic and Telegraphic Consultative Committee (CCITT) makes recommendations for serial protocols. These are identified by X. or V. prefixes. By far the most common choice for protocol at this time is the RS-232C standard. This specifies electrical, mechanical, and semantic standards for a 21-conductor serial communication interface. The CCITT V.24 recommendation is identical, except that the electrical signal characteristics are separately covered by the V.28 recommendation. The electrical characteristics essentially are greater than 5 V for logical 0 and less than -5 V for logical 1 on transmission, while receivers should discriminate signals outside of a 3 to -3 V range. The various signals carried by the principal conductors are illustrated in Figure 9.5 with pin assignments, EIA labels, and CCITT labels. This RS-232C standard, besides having a 10 V range between the two logic levels, also requires level transitions to occur within 4 percent of the single-bit transmission time. This high-speed switching

V.24 Signal

```
AA - Frame Ground          FG
AB - Signal Ground         SG
BA - Transmit Data         TD
CA - Ready To Send         RTS
CD - Data Terminal Ready   DTR
BB - Receive Data          RD
CB - Clear To Send         CTS
CC - Data Set Ready        DSR
CE - Ring Indicate         RI
CF - Carrier Detect        CD
```

Figure 9.5   V.24 interface.

requires very low capacitance in the transmission path, and therefore limits standard shielded cables to lengths less than about 15 m. Transmission speeds can range up to a maximum of 19.2 kbps (thousand bits per second) in specific steps, although 9.6 kbps is not often exceeded in practice. For a more complete discussion, see Witten [1983].

To improve upon deficiencies in the RS-232C standard, the EIA later developed the RS-449 standard (which was not specifically adopted by the CCITT). The electrical specifications for this standard are separately covered by RS-422A (V.11), or an optional RS-423A (V.10). RS-449 provides higher data transfer rates than the previous RS-232C standard, along with improved noise immunity. The RS-423A version is similar to RS-232C, except that the logic levels are separated by only 8V (still making it possible for an RS-232C receiver to accept these signals), the signal ground is only connected at the transmitter end (preventing errors due to differences in ground potentials), and a few more control circuits have been provided. Figure 9.6 shows how this standard compares to RS-232C.

```
V.10 Signal                    Equivalent V.24 Signal

SG - Signal Ground             AA - Frame Ground
SD - Send Data                 BA - Transmit Data
RS - Ready To Send             CA - Ready To Send
TR - Terminal Ready            CD - Data Terminal Ready
RD - Receive Data              BB - Receive Data
CS - Clear To Send             CB - Clear To Send
DM - Data Mode                 CC - Data Set Ready
RR - Receiver Ready            CF - Carrier Detect
IC - Incoming Call             CE - Ring Indicate
SC - Signal Common
RC - Receiver Common
IS - Terminal In Service
TT - Terminal Timing
ST - Send Timing
RT - Receive Timing
SQ - Signal Quality
NS - New Signal
SF - Select Frequency
SR - Signalling Rate
SI - Signalling Rate Indicator
LL - Local Loopback
RL - Remote Loopback
TM - Test Mode
SS - Select Standby
SB - Standby Indicate
```

Figure 9.6   V.10 and V.24 differences.

The RS-422A version of the RS-449 standard (try to keep all of these numbers straight) differs from the RS-423A version in that critical signal carrying conductors are now replaced by two conductors in a balanced transmission mode. The signal is indicated by the voltage difference between the two conductors, without any reference to the ground potential. This allows for the other difference from RS-423A, which is that the logic levels are now separated by only 800 mV. This makes it possible to power an RS-422A interface using the same voltages as used by computer circuits, namely 5 and -5 V, while the RS-232C standard requires an additional power supply to provide its voltage levels. The RS-449 standards are capable of transmitting data over distances in excess of 1 km: the RS-422A at 100 kbps, the RS-423A at 1 kbps. The conductors marked by an asterisk in Figure 9.7 are the ones which are replaced by balanced pairs in RS-422A.

Both versions of RS-449 have well in excess of 40 conductors in their cables. This is as a result of pressing analog circuits to perform a basically digital function. The CCITT has banked on a future when digital communication will be used throughout, including the entire phone network. The telecommunications industry is also working towards this goal with integrated service digital networks (ISDN). In this environment, telephone systems would be entirely digital—from jack to jack. Constructing LANs would be as simple as plugging nodes into telephone wall jacks. Data transmission rates of up to 64 kbps are expected, compared to the 1.2 or 2.4 kbps now achievable with modems.

To this end, the CCITT has developed the X.21 recommendation for digital serial communications, at a minimum transmission rate of 56 kbps. The electrical

```
Balanced           V.10 Signal


               SG - Signal Ground
      *        SD - Send Data
      *        RS - Ready To Send
      *        TR - Terminal Ready
      *        RD - Receive Data
      *        CS - Clear To Send
      *        DM - Data Mode
      *        RR - Receiver Ready
               IC - Incoming Call
               SC - Signal Common
               RC - Receiver Common
               IS - Terminal In Service
      *        TT - Terminal Timing
      *        ST - Send Timing
      *        RT - Receive Timing
               SQ - Signal Quality
               NS - New Signal
               SF - Select Frequency
               SR - Signalling Rate
               SI - Signalling Rate Indicator
               LL - Local Loopback
               RL - Remote Loopback
               TM - Test Mode
               SS - Select Standby
               SB - Standby Indicate
```

Figure 9.7   Balanced conductors in V.10

characteristics are defined under X.26 (similar to RS-423A) and X.27 (similar to RS-422A). This standard uses only eight conductors to pass data and control information between devices, as illustrated in Figure 9.8. All data traveling over this interface are in digital form, including dial tones and protocol signals. This standard also serves as the physical level of the X.25 packet-switching interface which is the subject of the following section.

9.3.2 Wide Area Networks

Wide area networks (WANs) are the extension of LAN concepts to larger scales. Here, individual nodes on a network may be separated by regional, national, or international distances. Individual nodes consist of full computer systems or entire LANs themselves (accessed by the communication servers mentioned in Section 9.1). The networks are most commonly built from existing telecommunications network systems of telephone-switching offices, trunk cables, microwave links, and satellite links.

The communication protocol most commonly employed for this purpose is a packet switching protocol. In such a system, data to be transmitted are split into fixed size packets by a processor known as a Packet Assembler/Disassembler (PAD). These packets are individually addressed to the destination node in a form suitable for the telecommunication system and transmitted through the network. On arrival at their destination, the packets are reassembled into the message by another PAD. The message is then sent from the PAD to the receiving computer system.

The governing standard for packet switching systems is the CCITT X.25 recommendation. It consists of several individual recommendations that cover various aspects of the computer-to-PAD-to-network interface. As mentioned earlier, X.21 covers the physical signaling between the computer and the PAD. X.26 and X.27 cover the electrical characteristics of the computer/PAD and PAD/network interfaces in a manner similar to V.10 and V.11 discussed previously.

```
                    X.21 Signal

          Common:

             G - Ground

          Data Terminal Equipment (DTE):

             T - Transport
             C - Control
            Ga - DTE Common

          Data Communication Equipment:

             R - Receive
             I - Indicate
             S - Signal (bit timing)
             B - Byte Timing
```

Figure 9.8   X.21 interface.

X.3—Parameters of PAD (the major parameters)

Parm Meaning		Values	
1	may user escape to parameter-change mode	0, 1	boolean
2	should PAD echo characters to terminal	0, 1	boolean
3	when should PAD send partial packets	0	never
		1	on <cr>
		126	on a ¬char
4	timeout for partial packet filling	0–255	(in 50 ms ticks)
5	may PAD inhibit terminal sending	0, 1	boolean
6	may PAD send service signals to terminal	0, 1	boolean
7	what should PAD do on <break> key	0	ignore
		1	interrupt
		2	reset self
		4	send a control packet to host
		8	escape to parameter mode
		16	discard current packet
8	should PAD discard host output sent to terminal	0, 1	boolean
9	number of filler characters to send after a <cr >	0–7	chars
10	automatic line fold length	0–255	chars
11	speed of terminal (bps)	0	110
		1	134.5
		2	300
		8	200
		9	100
		10	50
12	may terminal inhibit PAD from sending a packet	0, 1	boolean

The X.25 standard applies to the interface between host computers and the network; the interface from dumb terminals to the network is separately covered under the less complex X.3 and its interface characteristics standards X.28 and X.29.

PROBLEMS

9.1 A serial data transfer is happening at 2,400 bit/second. The transfer is using eight data bits, an even parity bit, and two stop bits for each character transferred. What is the effective data transfer rate of meaningful bits/second (baud rate), not including the start bit, parity bit, and stop bits? What percent of the data stream is meaningful?

9.2 Design a neutral file format and coding scheme to support point and line entities in 3D. How would you structure the file? What kind of overhead information needs to be included in the file? How can you balance conciseness in the file size against the ease of interpretation?

part three

Selection, Implementation, and Management of CAD Systems

This section of the book examines the methods by which CAD technology may be brought into an organization. Chapter 10 discusses how an appropriate CAD system for a particular application and organization may be selected. The system capabilities discussed in Part One are used to provide criteria for the evaluation of the functionality of various CAD systems, while the CIM considerations of Part Two are used to provide an appropriate context for system evaluation. Methods of day-to-day management of the CAD system are also discussed in Chapter 10, with insights gathered from many managers of CAD facilities in established industries. Finally, Chapter 11 examines the use of CAD technology by one particular organization in detail. Parallels are then drawn between the actual use of the CAD system and the methods outlined in this section.

chapter 10

SELECTING AND RUNNING THE CAD SYSTEM

The first problem to contend with when attempting to bring computer-aided design technology to an organization is the selection of an appropriate system. The new CAD manager must determine a set of appropriate selection criteria, solicit information from various sources, sort through the resulting mass of paper, and subsequently evaluate and rank the many available systems. In short, managers must identify their needs, determine the functionality of the various systems, and make comparisons between them.

There is a set of basic features that should be found on every CAD system being considered. This includes interactive computer graphics, common design and manufacturing database, and manufacturing software (such as NC programming, CAPP, and so forth). Any system which does not provide this minimum functionality can be trivially rejected. The selection task then becomes one of determining which system provides the best form of these functions, with additional desirable functions, at the lowest cost—essentially a cost/benefit analysis.

10.1 SYSTEM SELECTION PROCESS

The selection of the best CAD system for use in an organization can be a formidable task. The range of capabilities offered by the various vendors is wide, with equally wide variations in relative strengths and weaknesses. However, an intelligent choice can be made through a systematic approach. This section presents a simple five-step approach to the selection of the most appropriate CAD system for a particular organization.

The first step is to identify the needs that the CAD system is expected to meet. The manager making this decision should be sure to solicit input from all related areas of the organization to arrive at a clear and complete list. Design engineering, manufacturing engineering, finance, and the MIS department will all have their own views on the requirements of the CAD system. These should all be accounted for.

Second, the identified needs are translated into a set of CAD functional requirements that are necessary to meet the needs. These functional requirements can then be used as criteria for system evaluation, as they are typically quantifiable features of a CAD system.

Next, the manager should gather all available information on the CAD systems in the market. This includes information supplied by vendors, by user groups, and through visits to other companies using CAD in related applications. This later source may also provide information that can be used to further refine the list of identified needs.

Using the established evaluation criteria and the information gathered, the manager can then rank the various systems on their abilities to meet the identified needs. Through this evaluation, a short list of candidate systems can be formed. Only systems that are closely ranked near the top of the list should be included.

Finally, the vendors of these systems should then be invited to participate in benchmark tests. These benchmarks serve as a method of observing the different systems performing tasks similar to the tasks to be encountered in normal operation in the organization. The system performing best in the benchmark tests becomes the final selection.

10.1.1 Identifying Needs

The most important step in selecting an appropriate CAD system for any application is to have a clear and complete view of the exact needs it is to fill. These needs can then be translated into a set of particular functional requirements of the system. These functional requirements will subsequently serve as the evaluation criteria for comparing the various systems available.

Simply generating a list of needs to be met by the CAD system is not sufficient, however. These needs must be appropriately ordered so that priority can be given to meeting crucial needs over less important needs. There should be a clear distinction between needs that must be completely met by a system, needs that are significant but not essential, and needs that are nonessential value-added features.

Before progressing to comparing the various functional capabilities of the available systems, managers must identify their needs in terms of system abilities, system reliability, and performance requirements. Some particular factors that might be considered in determining these needs follow. Another useful list can be found in Groover [1984].

Cost:
  Hardware
  Software
  Hardware Maintenance
  Software Upgrades
  Documentation
  Training Programs

Customer Responsiveness:
  Field Service
  Response Time
  Parts Availability
  Software Bug Fixes

Performance:
  Number of Workstations Supported
  System Response Time (typical, heavy load)
  System Crash Recovery
  Peripheral Device Speed
  Ergonomic Considerations
  Communications Interfaces

Product Quality:
  Corporate Stability and Reputation
  Hardware Reliability
  Documentation Completeness and Accuracy
  Service Expertise and Response
  User Groups

Delivery and Postsales Support:
  Installation Assistance
  In-House Benchmarks
  Thorough Acceptance Checks

Software Features:
  User Programming Language
  System Management Software
  Usage Logging
  Add-On Packages (CAE, and so on)
  Application Specific Software (PCB design, piping, plant design, and so on)

Functionality of systems

Having established a clear set of needs to be met by the CAD system, the manager can proceed to reformulate this information into a set of functional requirements of the system. This is done by determining the particular CAD functions required to meet each identified need. These functional requirements can then serve as evaluation criteria for system comparisons.

The goal of Part One of this book is to provide sufficient background on the functions of CAD systems to enable a manager to carry out this reformulation. It covers the range of the features available on CAD systems through which the system can meet the needs of the organization. These features may be used as criteria to aid in the evaluation of different systems. Some of these features are:

- types of entities supported
- degree of attribute support
- degree of pattern support
- degree of user control over drafting entity parameters
- range of manipulation and transformation operations
- two- or three-dimensional modeling
- types of splines and surfaces provided
- solid modeling ability
- shading ability and method used
- support of macros
- support of a user programming language
- sophistication of the user programming language
- finite element modeling
- kinematic analysis
- simulation abilities
- NC programming methods
- hardware communications methods

It is important to realize that no system has all of these features in their ideal form. Managers must correlate their identified needs with the system functions and features that can best meet those needs. This correlation will serve as a translation from their identified application needs to a set of required features of the chosen system. For example, an application need for easy visualization of complex 3D shapes may translate into a system requirement for Gouraud shading ability. This set of required features then provides the manager with a basis for performing intelligent and systematic comparisons between various CAD systems.

10.1.2 Ergonomics in CAD/CAM

Under the heading of ergonomics are those factors that affect the interfacing between the CAD system and its human operators. This includes physical attributes of the system such as input devices and display designs, and environmental and procedural aspects such as equipment layout and work schedules. In computer-aided design, there is a close working relationship between the human users and the interface of the computer system. The effectiveness of this relation in transferring information between operator and computer is critical to the efficient running of the system. Ergonomics applied to the design of the CAD system and to its implementation in the company will insure the effectiveness of information transfer and the resulting efficiency of the system. The ergonomic factors of a particular terminal design are beyond the control of the manager implementing the CAD system. However, they can be used to rate the various terminals available as options from each particular vendor, and to rate the differences between vendors.

The first factor to consider in terminal design is the display. It is the primary source of information for the operator about the status of the design, both from display graphics and from text messages from the system. There are many factors in recognizing a well-designed display screen from an ergonomic viewpoint. The screen size should be large enough to display a significant portion of a part while maintaining a clear display of details. Screens much smaller than 19 inches do not serve this need well. The screen should also have operator controls for varying brightness and contrast. This allows users to set the brightness and contrast to levels that they feel appropriate for changing environmental lighting conditions.

The advantages of using color screens for displaying information are well known. In deciphering and understanding a complex 3D CAD model displayed on the screen, color becomes essential. The use of monochromatic screens will seriously impair the productivity of the system users.

After the screen, the next major component in the terminal is the keyboard. Fortunately, keyboard design has been somewhat standardized, although there are various options available. A separate keypad for numeric data entry is a particularly useful example of such an option, as is a set of user-programmable function keys.

One other input device that should be given special consideration is the lightpen. Its inclusion by CAD vendors is becoming more common. This is unfortunate. Although the lightpen provides a fast access to all locations on the screen, it suffers from several deficiencies. First is its lack of precision. This precision is limited by the size of the aperture in the tip of the pen, and by parallax effects caused by the thickness of the glass at the face of the screen.

Another serious problem is the significant user fatigue that can be experienced using the lightpen. This is due to the vertical arrangement of the screen face which requires the user to hold the lightpen and his or her arm up for extended periods. This one difficulty could be eased by placing the screen in a relatively horizontal arrangement, so that the pen may be rested on its face.

The cable attachment of the lightpen to the terminal is also inconvenient to work with. It clutters the work area immediately in front of the user. However, this may be corrected by the development of cordless lightpens.

Besides helping to recognize effective terminal designs, ergonomics can also play a significant role in the design of an effective layout for a workstation (this being the CAD terminal, associated work surfaces and desktops, and the ambient environmental conditions). One facet of this role is in the identification of certain preferable spatial relations between parts of the workstation that research has determined. For example, the following data have been determined as optimal for the arrangement of some components in the workstation [Dreyfuss 1959 and Kroener 1983]:

> Viewing Angle (from eye to screen):
> 15°–30° below horizontal
> Keyboard Angle:
> raised 11°–15°
> Table Height:
> adjustable in 700–780 mm range
> Screen Distance (from eye):
> 330 mm minimum, 350–450 mm typical

Lighting level is another important consideration in creating a comfortable environment for the CAD users, in which they can work at maximum productivity. Typically, illumination levels of 1,600 lux or more are recommended for office environments. This may be excessive for workstations, as levels in excess of 1,000 lux are apt to cause distracting glare on the workstation screens. A superior design would use slightly lower ambient illumination levels supplemented by adequate task lighting for the work surfaces. The glare problem can also be countered by the appropriate placement of the luminaires. Insuring that luminaires are placed more than 55 degrees above the line of sight will greatly reduce the problem of direct glare [Megaw 1983].

10.1.3 Comparing Systems

After clearly identifying needs and researching the various CAD systems available in the market, the manager must make a selection. One relatively straightforward method of using the collected information to help make this selection is to use ranking. In this method, the selection criteria are first established, using the guidelines set out previously. The individual criteria are given rankings (perhaps on a simple 1-to-10 scale) to reflect their relative importance. Then, each of the systems under consideration is given a ranking of its performance with respect to each criterion. The overall ranking of any one system is the aggregate total of the individual rank of the system with respect to a particular criterion, multiplied by that criterion's overall rank. The system receiving the highest overall ranking is the system to be selected.

For example, compare two systems A and B. The criteria used and their relative rankings are: meeting minimum needs (10), future expandability towards

CIM (8), additional functionality (4), ergonomic design (7). The systems might be evaluated as shown below:

Criterion	System A	System B
min. needs	9	8
expansion	6	8
functions	9	6
ergonomics	5	7

The aggregate scores for the two systems would then be

$$\text{System A} = 10(9) + 8(6) + 4(9) + 7(5) = 209$$

$$\text{System B} = 10(8) + 8(8) + 4(6) + 7(7) = 217$$

In this example, system B is determined to be the superior choice since it has the higher aggregate score. This is in spite of it having a lower individual score on the minimum needs criterion, the most important criterion.

In the example, each system is given a score in each of the criteria which reflects its relative ability to fully meet the needs represented by the evaluation criteria. This is done by studying the information gathered on each system under consideration. The criteria themselves were also ranked to reflect the relative importance of each criterion to the overall purchase decision. Crucial criteria are given high rankings, while lesser criteria are given lower rankings. As previously explained, these rankings are determined by prioritizing the particular needs that the system is to meet, and subsequently relating these needs to particular evaluation criteria. The CAD functions that are required to meet high-priority needs receive correspondingly high criterion rankings.

10.2 JUSTIFYING CAD/CAM

Justifying the expense of a CAD/CAM system can be a difficult enterprise. The usual approach is to consider the CAD system as another piece of equipment that will simply result in a certain productivity gain in design and manufacturing, and thereby yield a certain cost improvement. Although the productivity gains that may be realized with a well-managed CAD/CAM system can be substantial, justifications based on the traditional approach often fail. This is primarily due to the failure of the traditional cost accounting measures to fully reflect the total benefits of CAD/CAM, especially when it serves as an element in an overall CIM strategy. This section examines how to expand common accounting procedures to see the true effects of the installation of the system.

The traditional approach

The traditional methods of accounting are often seen as inappropriate for evaluating CAD/CAM and other strategic high-technology projects. However, in most companies, attempting a traditional cost justification is still a necessary evil. Typically, the CAD/CAM manager might proceed along the following lines adapted from Culley [1985]:

(Reprinted by permission of the Council of the Institution of Mechanical Engineers from "Justifying CADCAM–the Steps")

1. Identifying the functions of the various departments in the company. This is necessary because the operation of the new CAD/CAM system may have impact that cuts across many departmental boundaries.

2. Furthering this analysis by identifying individual job elements and subtasks in the departments most closely related to the new system.

3. Determining and applying the direct savings that are attributable to the productivity gains expected. Note that because of the wide impact of the new technology, these savings will be greater the larger the scope of view taken.

4. Applying related savings that will arrive in other areas, such as from processes that will become redundant or irrelevant.

5. Determining the impact of these projected savings on the financial state of the company.

6. Performing a cash-flow analysis to determine either the payback or the expected return on investment, depending on the methods endorsed in the company.

7. Finally, remembering to consider the impact of the system on lead times and other intangibles.

Problems with the traditional approach

There are a number of difficulties with this traditional cost-justification approach when it is applied to high-technology projects in general and strategic goals, such as CIM, in particular. These difficulties are now examined more closely. This section is largely drawn from the report of the Canadian CAD/CAM Council [1976], where a more complete discussion of these difficulties can be found (reprinted with permission).

Traditional cost accounting does not sufficiently reveal the benefits of automation. Experienced automation users have found that gains often came from unexpected or misunderstood sources, rather than from factors identified in cost justifications. Frequently, those factors considered in cost justifications did not achieve their expected payoffs.

Traditional cost accounting also does not allow for the separation of overhead on a functional basis, such as expediting costs or entry-error costs, to more clearly identify costs that may be reduced by automation. For this reason, CIM-related projects stand a better chance of being seen in a cost-effective light the larger the view taken when evaluating them.

Most CIM-related projects, with CAD/CAM in particular, find their major cost improvements in overhead reductions and improvements in nonquantifiables. Some of these nonquantifiable benefits of CAD/CAM are [Beeby 1986]:

Increased adaptability to market changes

More predictable schedules

Less duplication of engineering data for manufacturing use

Fewer unplanned manufacturing revisions

Availability of NC data for use in quality control

Close to 85 percent of the benefits gained from CAD/CAM are in these nonquantifiables. As these benefits also affect profit, and thereby return on investment, they should be given more appropriate weighting in the analysis.

Companies that operate on a profit center basis may find it especially difficult to justify automation costs because overly restricted and narrow results may become the sole basis of evaluation. For CIM and related technologies, the benefits are to a large extent felt outside of the immediate center of implementation. The profit center approach often leads to islands of automation with redundant features and underutilized capacity. A strategic approach for the entire company is required to keep the walls between centers from becoming higher.

Finally, in some companies CAD/CAM and other automation technologies may not be justifiable on a cost basis at all, but can be justified as strategic decisions. It is important to also consider the cost of not implementing automation technologies, such as the cost of orders lost to competitors who can deliver better quality in shorter delivery times through their use of CAD/CAM in a CIM environment. As in the aphorism, "the factory of the future is the factory with a future."

10.3 CAD/CAM MANAGEMENT

Having received a commitment from top management to move towards CIM, and having selected and installed the most appropriate system in a proper environment, the manager is now prepared to begin the day-to-day operation of the CAD/CAM facility. Part One of this book has provided managers with a complete background of the functional abilities of the CAD system, without the extensive time requirement for learning the intricate details to the operation of the CAD workstations. Part Two has complemented this by providing insight into how the CAD/CAM facility should fit into an overall CIM strategy and philosophy of operation. The first part of this present section has illustrated how to select and implement an effective and productive system. It now remains only to ensure the continued smooth running of the facility and the steady progression towards full computer-integrated manufacturing.

As operation of the computer-based facility proceeds, the manager should become aware of the increasing importance of maintaining the integrity of the

CAD/CAM database. A significant investment in engineering and design has been made in order to develop the information stored in the computer files, so appropriate attention should be paid to protecting that investment. Security measures should be taken that are in line with the value of the data.

First in security measures to be implemented is control over access to the system. This includes physical access and logical access. Physical access is controlled by limiting access to the rooms where certain key components of the system are located. In order of increasing need for security, these components are the user workstations, the system operator console, and the physical computer (CPU and magnetic tapes). Logical access to the system is insured by the use of userids and passwords. This information should be distributed on a strict need-to-know basis only. This insures that only authorized users of the system can gain access to it.

Next in the security measures is the establishment of protection classes for files and user classes for userids. This will prevent casual users of the system from accidental modification or deletion of critical system files. It also provides a mechanism for controlling the availability of information to different classes of users. This provides the system manager with a method of gating manufacturing access to part files pending their completion by design engineering.

Finally, the most visible means of preserving data integrity and insuring the security of critical data and work in progress is the data backup procedure. This involves making copies of important data files on a regular basis and storing the copies remote from the system. This serves two needs. First, it provides a method of recovering valuable data in the event of catastrophic system failure, such as a disk head crash or a fire. Second, and more frequently, it provides a method of restoring files accidentally modified or deleted by users. It is because of this second use that backups of user files should be made on a daily basis. One typical system backup scheme is as follows:

1. *Daily*: Make backup copies of all files that have been modified in the previous 24 hours. Most operating systems have provisions for tracking modification dates and times. The tapes used for this may be reused on a rotating seven-tape basis.

2. *Weekly:* Make backup copies of all files modified in the previous week. Use a rotating four-tape system.

3. *Monthly:* Make a full backup of all user files, including all user classes and protection classes. Permanently store this tape in a safe location.

Under this system, a catastrophic system failure can be recovered from by sequentially restoring the latest monthly backup, the weekly backups made since the monthly backup was performed, and the daily backups made since the last weekly backup was made. In the worst case, only 24 hours worth of development may be lost.

Avoiding common pitfalls

Finally, there are a number of common pitfalls that the manager may encounter when implementing a CAD/CAM system and its associated policies and procedures. These points are the accumulated knowledge of many managers who have installed new CAD/CAM facilities and have lived to tell the tale. Some of their problems have been costly, and some have been subtle and difficult to identify. Don't repeat their mistakes. Use these points as guidelines in implementing a cost-effective and smoothly running CAD/CAM facility in your organization.

1. Do not try to run the installation in a half-electronic, half-paper mode in a misguided attempt to "ease into" the new technology. Go all or none when computerizing the facility. Don't waste time and energy switching between formats during a job.

2. Do not draft on the CAD system to create electronic blueprints and then manually create NC programs from them. A CAD system is a very expensive way of creating blueprints, which is only marginally faster than a skilled draftsman and pencil. Fully model the part on the system, and then use the full system capabilities in NC program generation.

3. Develop an interface between the CAD system and the corporate computer system that can be used to transfer status and planning information.

4. Develop CAD software in a stepwise manner, from keystroke macros, to small programs and procedures written in a user programming language, to large programs and systems. It is the development of company-specific custom software that provides true increases in CAD productivity. Without such software, a return on investment for any CAD system may take a long time.

5. Use commercially available software wherever possible. Use in-house development only for highly specialized applications.

6. Do not use hardcopy plots as your final product. Remain in an electronic form wherever possible. Again, this is to reduce wasted time and effort in changing formats.

7. Protect your work in progress. Always make backups, whether on tape, disk, or cartridge. A minimum backup scheme would include rotating daily, rotating weekly, and permanent monthly backups.

8. Allow sufficient training and exploration time for designers learning the system. As a guideline, allow six months to one year for new graduates, one to two years for experienced draftsmen and designers to achieve full productivity on the new system. Remember, your experienced personnel will have to unlearn their old manual techniques before they can fully learn the new CAD system techniques.

9. Remember the human factors of CAD/CAM work. Working on a CAD terminal is very intense. Frequent breaks, as well as a properly designed environment, are necessary for keeping designers at their top productivity.

10. Try to deal with your suppliers and customers in an entirely electronic form. Direct connection or dialup file transfer is best. In lieu of that, exchange magnetic tapes containing CAD files in a neutral format.

11. Have systems programmers and software designers solicit input from designers, NC programmers, and all other users of the CAD/CAM system. These people will know best where their tasks can benefit from automated tools and processes.

12. Strive to achieve and maintain an open database format. Remain in the most flexible form to facilitate your eventual implementation of a complete CIM environment.

13. Use group technology methods to take advantage of the similarities between parts and between manufacturing processes.

14. Time the introduction of new technology and moves towards CIM carefully. A "wait and see" attitude can be costly as competitors progress through the learning curve and sooner gain the competitive advantage of the new technologies. The strategic cost of not beginning CAD application may be much higher than the costs of implementing these new computer-based technologies.

15. Track changes in productivity in each area of the operation. This allows the identification of bottlenecks and of areas where further expansion may be justified.

16. Get involved in the new technology. Its successful implementation depends more on the skills and knowledge of managers than on the particular equipment.

chapter 11

Case Study in Selection and Implementation

11.1 THE ORGANIZATION

Tradesco Mold Limited of Toronto, Ontario is a small to mid-sized manufacturing firm involved in the design and manufacture of injection molds for plastic parts. The Tradesco organization was founded in 1976 and currently employs approximately 100 people in its mold production. Besides complete molds for plastic part manufacture, Tradesco also produces individual mold components for repairs and retrofits, provides mold engineering services, and repairs and refurbishes finished molds.

Recently, Tradesco began an expansion of its facilities. The establishment of a sister company in New Brunswick with expanded design and manufacturing operations significantly increased the mold production capacity, and increased the resulting demands to be placed on any CAD system to be used.

11.2 INJECTION MOLD MAKING

Injection molds are complex mechanisms containing hundreds of intricate and closely toleranced parts. They contain electrically heated manifolds for the delivery of molten plastic resin to the part cavities, complex water and air-cooling systems, as well as internal mechanisms to control the ejection of solidified parts after the mold opens. The part cavities involve complex 3D surfaces, often with dimensional tolerances as tight as 0.005 mm. The mold components are manufactured from a wide variety of steels and other metals selected for hardness, wear resistance, and fracture toughness. The machining requirements are often very demanding. Figure 11.1 illustrates the complexity of some injection mold parts.

The mold design begins with the specification of the finished part requirements by the customer. This plastic part is then scaled up by factors to account for the shrinkage that will occur as the resin solidifies in the mold. This expanded version of the part then serves as the specification for the molding surface of the part cavities. The stack components, which are the components that close to form the part cavity, can then be designed. The design of the stack components will necessarily place a number of functional requirements on the other parts of the mold. These requirements place restrictions on the design of the remaining parts of the mold, such as the manifold design, and the air and water layout in the supporting mold plates. From these requirements, and from requirements of the machine in which the mold will be used, the mold shoe can be designed. The mold shoe refers to the nonstack parts of the mold, such as the mold plates and mechanisms.

After the design is completed, the manufacturing process begins. Based on the design drawings, and on the bill of materials produced, materials can be purchased, stock items can be obtained, and planning for the machining of nonstock components can begin. Process plans are developed for the manufacture of the individual components, NC programs are created for the various component and machine combinations required, and the job is placed in the manufacturing shop

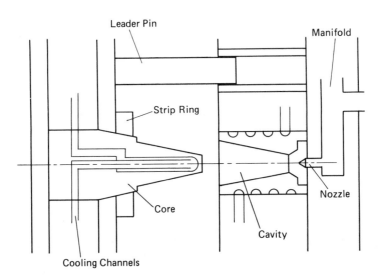

Figure 11.1   Mold components.

schedule. When manufacturing is complete, the finished components are quality inspected, assembled into a complete mold, and tested by producing plastic parts. Typically, these parts are then inspected by the customers, who then give their final acceptance of the mold.

11.3 CAD APPLICATION

In looking to improve the productivity of its mold manufacturing operation, Tradesco realized the capabilities of CAD and its related technologies to facilitate many of the design and manufacturing engineering tasks. A properly selected and implemented CAD system could be used to achieve significant productivity gains in many areas. In design, CAD may be used to facilitate the design of parts, the application of shrinkage factors, the determination of optimal gate locations, and the design and detailing of stack and shoe components. Sophisticated analyses may be performed on resin flows, heat distributions, and component stresses, while macros and user programs may be used to detail stack components and modify standard shoe components. In manufacturing, the CAD data may be used to automatically generate bills of material. The CAD system may also be used to generate toolpaths for the machining of molding surfaces or entire components. These toolpaths are then processed into the NC programs that will control the machining process.

Tradesco management fully recognized the advantages that can be had through the use of CAD technology in their operations. In 1985, they installed a CAD system to assist with the design engineering process. This system was used in the production of approximately 30 percent of the molds manufactured each year. With the expansion of their facilities and the increase in production, Tradesco managers realized that a larger and more powerful CAD system would be required. Thus, they began the process of selecting and installing a new successor system.

Prior to the selecting and installing of the new CAD system, Tradesco staff made a careful analysis of the feasibility and financial acceptability of the new technology. A cost justification was performed to consider the viability of implementing a multistation CAD system for use in part and mold design, and with the potential for future use in the areas of part modeling and analysis. This initial study identified reduced lead times and greater flexibility as the areas from which the primary benefits would be realized. These gains were expected to offset the initial capital outlay and the operational costs of the system. After operating the system for a number of months, it was discovered that additional gains were also being realized in the simplification of, and the faster response to, design changes.

11.3.1 The System Selection

As explained in Chapter 10, the process for selecting an appropriate CAD system consists of three distinct phases: recognizing the requirements of the expected applications, establishing criteria for evaluation, and performing the evaluation of prospective systems.

CAD technology has several obvious application areas in mold design and manufacture. Some of the primary applications are:

part design
part detail drafting
resin flow analysis and modeling
stack design
component detailing and drafting
toolpath generation
computer generation of bills of material

From these applications, Tradesco was able to select those which were relevant to their application, and from them to identify the requirements of a selected CAD system. Some applications, such as the creation of detailed component drawings, were viewed as essential in the Tradesco operation, while others, such as 3D modeling of parts, were considered primarily as areas of future development.

With a defined set of requirements of the system, criteria for evaluating prospective CAD systems could then be established. The primary criteria used by Tradesco in selecting their new system were:

- the production of excellent quality detail drawings
- fully featured dimensioning and annotating capabilities
- stable vendor with established client base and support system
- competitive pricing
- electronic links to remote workstations at other sites
- ability to add NC and process planning at a later date
- ability to add shading and solid modeling at a later date
- ability to add user programming at a later date

11.3.2 The System

The evaluation of potential systems was carried out by Tradesco and a team of consultants and researchers from the University of Toronto, Department of Mechanical Engineering. The evaluation process initially narrowed the choices to three computer hardware vendors and three CAD software developers.

Further evaluation led to the final selection of a system of Auto-Trol CAD software and Empress/32 database software running on Apollo workstations. Its overall performance in the identified criteria was felt to be sufficient to make it an excellent choice for the Tradesco implementation. The selected system software consists of Auto-Trol Series 7000 software. It is supported by a hardware platform consisting of seven Apollo 3500 workstations connected through the Apollo Domain token ring LAN. Six of the workstations are used for mold design, while one is currently used for manufacturing planning and control. Dedicated phone lines are planned to link a similar facility at the sister plant.

11.3.3 The Implementation Process

The successful management of the new CAD facility has required the formulation of new specific management and operational techniques. A comprehensive training program was established with the system vendor, through which tailored training courses were provided for Tradesco employees. Overview and system management courses were provided for Tradesco managers, while detail system usage courses were provided for the designers now operating the CAD terminals.

Currently, the system is used for the design of most major components of the injection molds, and in shop floor control for the management of bills of material and shop orders. A group technology coding and classification scheme, developed by the same team of university consultants, is employed to take full advantage of the many similarities in the design and manufacture of mold parts.

In the future, Tradesco plans to expand the system use to include NC programming and process planning functions. The group technology methods will also be applied in these areas. Also, additional workstations may be added to the network to support business computing needs, such as inventory control and financial planning.

For the system users, Tradesco has provided an ergonomic working environment. This includes special attention given to the lighting levels and arrangements, and to the types of seating provided at the workstations.

In the day-to-day operation of the CAD system, Tradesco managers have not yet developed a full set of appropriate metrics for measuring and tracking the gains made through the introduction of CAD to their operations. Given the highly strategic nature of CAD development and application, and the resultant difficulty of fully measuring its effects, this shortcoming is hardly surprising. Still, for most effective use of the system, it should be addressed.

11.3.4 The Payoff

From its past experiences, Tradesco has already realized the gains that can be achieved through CAD technology. These include improved design quality, shorter lead times, and increased flexibility. With the new larger system in place, these benefits are expected to increase substantially. In addition, further gains are expected in part design and the production of complex mold assembly drawings. For the future, Tradesco sees the opportunity for increased use of CAD/CAM and related technologies in its operations, especially in the areas of part modeling, and the machining of complex 3D surfaces. Overall, the implementation of CAD in the mold design and manufacturing operations of Tradesco has been a very successful and economically worthwhile venture.

Cross Reference of Multiple Terms

This cross reference resolves many of the differences between the terminology used by different CAD system vendors. Terms used in this book are listed first, followed by equivalent terms used by different CAD vendors. Specific CAD systems included are CADDS4X, ANVIL-4000, Unigraphics II, and CATIA. There is considerable overlap in the use of terms, with a single term referring to quite different features on different systems. Care must be taken when evaluating CAD systems, to have a clear understanding of the meanings associated with the terms being used.

Absolute coordinates   Model coordinates, global coordinates.
Arc   Circle.
Blank   Erase, hide, noshow.
Crosshatching   Fill, pattern, shade.
Delete   Remove, erase.
Density   Weight, width.
Digitize   Point, locate.
Directory   Catalog, library, file.
Drawing   Layout.
Fast Font   Quick text.
Figure   Pattern, ditto, subpart, block.
File   Model.

Graphics cursor   Crosshairs, pointer.
Image   View.
Layer   Level, sheet.
Line font   Style, line type, texture.
Macro   Key file, execute file.
Note   Text.
Pick   Select, indicate.
Reference layer   Inactive layer, frozen layer.
Repaint   Refresh, clean, redraw.
Retrieve   Insert.
Sweep curve   Driven curve.
Text font   Character set, style.
Toolpath   NC set.
Trap region   Pick region, entity capture distance.
View   Detail.
Window   Fence.
Work coordinates   User coordinates, active coordinates, construction plane, local coordinates.
Work layer   Active layer, construction layer.

References

BEEBY W., AND COLLIER, P., "New Directions Through CAD/CAM," Society of Manufacturing Engineers (Dearborn 1986).

"CAD/CAM Application Note 25," Bell-Northern Research (Ottawa 1988).

"Management in Crisis: Implementing Computer Integrated Manufacturing in Canada," Canadian CAD/CAM Council for the Advancement of Computer Integrated Manufacturing, July 1986.

CROWLEY, R., "Let's Discuss CAD/CAM Integration," Modern Machine Shop, Dec. 1984.

CULLEY, S., "Justifying CADCAM—the Steps" in "Effective CADCAM 1985," IMechE Conference Publications 1985–7, July 1985.

DREYFUSS, H., "The Measure of Man," Whitney Library of Design (New York 1959).

FOLEY, J., "Interfaces for Advanced Computing," Scientific American, Oct. 1987, pp. 126–135.

————, AND VANDAM, A., "Fundamentals of Interactive Computer Graphics," Addison-Wesley Publishing Company (Reading 1982).

GROOVER, M., AND ZIMMER, E., "CAD/CAM: Computer-Aided Design and Manufacturing," Prentice-Hall, Inc. (Englewood Cliffs 1984).

HYER, N., "Management's Guide to Group Technology," Operations Management Review, 2(2), Winter 1984.

————, AND WEMMERLOV, U., "Group Technology Oriented Coding Systems: Structures, Applications, and Implementation," Production and Inventory Management, JAPICS, 2nd Quarter, 1985.

KROENER, K., "Engineering Anthropometry: Work Space and Equipment to Fit the User" in "The Physical Environment at Work," Oborne, D., and Groneberg, M., eds., John Wiley and Sons (Toronto 1983).

MEGAW, E., AND BELLAMY, L., "Illumination at Work" in "The Physical Environment at Work," Oborne, D., and Groneberg, M., eds., John Wiley and Sons (Toronto 1983).

OPITZ, H., "A Classification System to Describe Workpieces," Pergamon Press (Oxford 1970).

RENZ, W., "VDAFS: A Pragmatic Interface for the Exchange of Sculptured Surface Data" in "Product Data Interfaces in CAD/CAM Applications," Encarnacao, J., et al., eds., Springer-Verlag (Heidelberg 1986).

SNODGRASS, A., "Meeting the 'Change Management' Challenge," Manufacturing Engineering, Nov. 1987, p. CT-7.

THOMSON, V., AND GRAEFE, U., "CIM—a Manufacturing Paradigm," National Research Council Report DM-006, 1987.

TULKOFF, J., "Implementing a Computer Process Planning System Based on a Group Technology Classification and Coding Scheme," Industrial Engineering Conference Proceedings, IIE, Fall 1984.

VALLIERE, D., "Improving CAD Productivity Through User Programming Languages," Computer-Aided Design Engineering and Drafting, 1 s(25), Auerbach Publishers, Inc. (New York 1986).

WIESSFLOG, U., "Product Data Exchange: Design and Implementation of IGES Processors" in "Product Data Interfaces in CAD/CAM Applications," Encarnacao, J., et al., eds., Springer-Verlag (Heidelberg 1986).

WITTEN, I., "Welcome to the Standards Jungle," Byte, 8(2) Feb. 1983, pp. 146–178.

ZGORZELSKI, M., "Computer Integrated Manufacturing: Trends, Problems, Strategies," Society of Automotive Engineers (Warrendale, 1986).

ADDITIONAL REFERENCES

BARMACK, J., AND SINAIKO, H., "Human Factors in Computer Generated Graphic Displays," Institute for Defense Analyses Study 234, April (AD 636 170).

BEEBY, W., "Integrating Engineering and Manufacturing" in "Advances in CAD/CAM: Case Studies," Wang, P., ed., Kluwer Academic Publishers (Boston 1984).

BERNARD, J., AND ROBINSON, P., "Flexible Manufacturing Simulation," Autofact 6 Conference Proceedings (Anaheim 1984).

BUI-TUONG, P., "Illumination for Computer- Generated Pictures," Communications of ACM, 18(6) June 1975, pp. 311–317.

CANRAD, R., AND HULL, A., "The Preferred Layout for Numerical Data-Entry Keysets," Ergonomics, 11, pp. 165–173.

CLANCY, J., "Directions for Engineering Data Exchange for Computer Aided Design and Manufacturing" in "Advances in CAD/CAM: Case Studies," Wang, P., ed., Kluwer Academic Publishers (Boston 1984).

CLARKE, R., AND ROBINSON, D., "Effective Use of Finite Element Analysis Techniques Within an Integrated CADCAM System" in "Effective CADCAM 1985," IMechE Conference Publications 1985–7, July 1985.

CLOSE, D., "Status Report to Senior Management," Cad/Cam & Robotics, June 1987, pp. 102–109.

DEGREENE, K., "Man-Computer Interrelationships" in "Systems Psychology," Degreene, K., ed., McGraw-Hill Book Company (Toronto 1970).

ELGABRY, A., "Communicating Product Definition and Support Data in a CAE/CAD/CAM Environment," Autofact '85 Conference Proceedings (Detroit 1985).

ERISMAN, A., AND NEVES, K., "Advanced Computing for Manufacturing," Scientific American, October 1987, pp. 162–169.

GOURAUD, H., "Continuous Shading of Curved Surfaces," IEEE Transactions on Computers, C-20(6) June 1971, pp. 623–628.

GRABOWSKI, H., AND GLATZ, R., "Testing and Validation of IGES Processors" in "Product Data Interfaces in CAD/CAM Applications," Encarnacao, J., et al., eds., Springer-Verlag (Heidelberg 1986).

GRANDJEAN, E., "Fitting the Task to the Man: an Ergonomic Approach," Taylor & Francis, Ltd. (London 1969).

HALEVI, G., "The Role of Computers in Manufacturing Processes," John Wiley and Sons (Toronto 1980).

HATVANY, J., "The Distribution of Functions in Manufacturing Systems" in "Advances in Computer-Aided Manufacture," McPherson, D., ed., North-Holland Publishing Company (Amsterdam 1979).

HITOMI, K., "Manufacturing Systems Engineering: A Unified Approach to Manufacturing Technology and Production Management," Taylor & Francis, Ltd. (London 1979).

HOFFMANN, T., "Production: Management and Manufacturing Systems," Wadsworth Publishing Company, Inc. (Belmont 1971).

HOUTZEEL, A., AND BROWN, C., "A Management Overview of Group Technology" in "Group Technology at Work," Hyer, N., ed., Society of Manufacturing Engineers (Dearborn 1984).

HUGHES, D., AND MAULL, R., "Software—the Key to Computer Integrated Manufacture" in "Effective CADCAM 1985," IMechE Conference Publications 1985–7, July 1985.

KLEMMER, E., "Keyboard Entry," Applied Ergonomics, 2, pp. 2–6.

KOBRICK, J., AND FINE, B., "Climate in Human Performance" in "The Physical Environment at Work," Oborne, D., and Groenberg, M., eds., John Wiley and Sons (Toronto 1983).

KRYDER, M., "Data-Storage Technologies for Advanced Computing," Scientific American, Oct 1987, pp. 116–125.

KRYTER, K., et al., "Hazardous Exposure to Intermittent and Steady-State Noise," JASA, 39, pp. 451–464.

MADDOX, M., et al., "Font Comparisons for 5x7 Dot Matrix Characters," Human Factors, 19, pp. 89–93.

MARSH, J., "Information Management in Computer Aided Engineering" in "Effective CADCAM 1985," IMechE Conference Publications 1985–7, July 1985.

MAYER, R., "IGES: One Answer to the Problems of CAD Database Exchange," Byte, 12(6) June 1987, pp. 209–214.

MCCORMICK, E., "Human Factors Engineering," McGraw-Hill Book Company (New York 1970).

NEUMAN, W., AND SPROULL, R., "Principles of Interactive Computer Graphics," McGraw-Hill Book Company (New York 1979).

PASEMANN, K., "Interfaces for CAD Applications" in "Product Data Interfaces in CAD/CAM Applications," Encarnacao, J., et al., eds., Springer-Verlag (Heidelberg 1986).

PERRI, R., "Release Control, Configuration Management, Design Retrieval, and Remote Viewing of CAD Generated Product Data Definitions" in "Advances in CAD/CAM: Case Studies," Wang, P., ed., Kluwer Academic Publishers (Boston 1984).

PETERS, G., AND ADAMS, B., "These Three Criteria for Readable Panel Markings," Product Engineering, May 25, 30, pp. 55–57.

PRESSMAN, R., AND WILLIAMS, J., "Numerical Control and Computer-Aided Manufacturing," John Wiley and Sons (Toronto 1977).

RATLIFF, F., "Mach Bands: Quantitaive Studies on Neural Networks in the Retina," Holden-Day (San Francisco 1965).

SANDERS, M., AND MCCORMICK, E., "Human Factors in Engineering and Design," McGraw-Hill Book Company (New York 1987).

SCHULZ, J., "Applications and Benefits of CAD/CAM Data in the Manufacturing Environment" in "Advances in CAD/CAM: Case Studies," Wang, P., ed., Kluwer Academic Publishers (Boston 1984).

SHUSTER, R., "Progress in the Development of CAD/CAM Interfaces for Transfer of Product Definition Data" in "Product Data Interfaces in CAD/CAM Applications," Encarnacao, J., et al., eds., Springer-Verlag (Heidelberg 1986).

SIM, R., "The Redistribution of Machine Dependant Software Within a Direct Numerical Control Environment" in "Computer Languages for Numerical Control," Hatvany, J., ed., North-Holland Publishing Company (Amsterdam 1973).

SIMON, W., "The Numerical Control of Machine Tools," Edward Arnold (Publishers), Inc. (London 1973).

SLAUTTERBACK, W., "The Manufacturing Environment in the Year 2000," Autofact 6 Conference Proceedings (Anaheim 1984).

TANENBAUM, A., "Computer Networks," Prentice-Hall, Inc. (Englewood Cliffs 1981).

TUDOR, P., "CAPP—the Engineering Database" in "Effective CADCAM 1985," IMechE Conference Publications 1985–7, July 1985.

TULKOFF, J., "GT-based Generative Process Planning" in "Group Technology at Work," Hyer, N., ed., Society of Manufacturing Engineers (Dearborn 1984).

VALLIERE, D., AND LEE, J., "Artificial Intelligence in Manufacturing," Automation, May 1988, pp. 41–45.

VARTABEDIAN, A., "Developing a Graphic Set for Cathode Ray Tube Display Using a 7x9 Dot Pattern," Applied Ergonomics, 4, pp. 11–16.

VERNADAT, F., "A Conceptual Schema for a CIM Database," Autofact 6 Conference Proceedings (Anaheim 1984).

————, "Computer-Integrated Manufacturing: On the Database Aspect," 3rd Canadian CAD/CAM & Robotics Conference, Society of Manufacturing Engineers (Dearborn 1984).

WELLER, E., "Nontraditional Machining Processes," Society of Manufacturing Engineers (Dearborn 1984).

WILFERT, H., AND SEELAND, H., "CAD/CAM: Integration in the Automobile Industry" in "Product Data Interfaces in CAD/CAM Applications," Encarnacao, J., et al., eds., Springer-Verlag (Heidelberg 1986).

WILSON, J., "Integrated Manufacturing and the Central Role of CADCAM" in "Effective CADCAM 1985," IMechE Conference Publications 1985–7, July 1985.

INDEX

AI (*see* **Artificial intelligence**)
Analysis, 1, 3, 5, 20, 78, 92, 98, 163
   flow, 4, 163, 164
APT, 121, 122, 127
Arc, 35, 39, 70, 84
Artificial Intelligence (*see also* Expert
   systems), 63, 112, 127
Associate, 27, 45, 50, 53, 55
Attribute, 45, 47, 55, 58, 152

Backup, 158, 159
Baseband, 130
Bill of material, 4, 104, 162–65
Blank, 56, 69, 90
Blending function, 44, 72
Broadband, 130

CAPP (*see also* **Process planning**),
   99, 103, 108–12, 149

Centerline, 41
Chain, 27
Circle, 35, 38, 41, 70, 84
Classification scheme, 107, 165
Clipping, 67, 68
Color, 47, 48, 61, 88, 153
Command, 22–24
Computer, 3, 4, 20, 34, 78, 129, 158
   microcomputer, 20
Conic, 40, 85
Contention, 130
Continuity, 42
Controller, NC, 117, 118, 122, 127
Convex hull property, 42, 72
Coordinates, 25, 26, 35, 41, 66, 67, 69,
   87, 88
   work, 66, 68
   absolute, 66, 70, 88
Copy option, 58, 89
Cost justification, 156, 163

Costs, 97, 98, 102, 130, 151, 155, 157, 160
Criteria (*see* Selection criteria)
Crosshatch, 53, 86
Cursor, 12, 14–16, 24–27, 83

Database, 55, 98–105, 149, 158, 160, 164
Datacassette, 19
DataGlove, 18
Density, Line, 47, 88
Dimensions, 5, 50–53, 55, 69
Directory, 28, 29
  hierarchy, 28
  root, 28, 29
  working, 29
Discrimination, 47, 48
Disk, 18, 19, 117, 129, 131, 158
DNC (*see also* Numerical control), 117
Drag, 57

Encoder, 115, 116
Ergonomics, 22, 152–54, 165
Expert systems (*see also* Artificial intelligence), 63, 112

FEM (*see* Finite element)
Figure, 54, 87
  part, 46, 53, 87
  pattern, 53, 55, 87
File, 28, 55, 90
  scratch, 32
Fillet, 39, 71, 84
Finite element, 92, 152
Font, 47, 48, 88
Function key (*see also* Keyboard), 12, 23, 79, 153

Graphics, 1, 3, 5

Gravity field, 26, 27
Grid, 25
Group, 27, 41, 47, 53, 85
Group Technology, 96, 98, 103, 104, 106, 107, 112, 160, 165

Hierarchy, Directory, 28
Highlight, 47
Hull, Convex, 48, 72

IGES, 136–43
Installation, 96, 130
Instance, 53, 54
Inventory, 99, 165
ISDN, 145

Joystick, 14

Keyboard, 12, 23, 79, 82, 153
  function, 12, 23, 79, 153
Kinematics, 92, 93, 152

Label, 49, 55, 70, 85
LAN (*see* Local area networks)
Layer, 47
  work, 47, 53, 88
Layout, 32, 67–69
Lightpen, 15, 153
Line, 24, 35, 36, 70, 84
Local area networks, 21, 129–35, 165
Locate, 12, 14, 22, 24, 25, 35, 37, 41
  lightpen (*see* Relocating algorithm)

Machine, NC, 117
Magnetic tape (*see also* Tape), 5, 18, 129, 158

Manufacturing, 3, 5, 65, 96, 97, 99, 104, 106, 108, 161, 163
  Flexible Manufacturing System, 99
MAP (*see also* Standards), 132
Mask, 27, 46–48
Material, Bill of (*see* Bill of material)
Matrix, 58, 59, 89
Medium, 130
Menu, 12, 22–24, 79
Mirror, 58, 89
Modeling, 5, 8, 59, 65, 152, 163, 164, 166
Monocode, 108
Mouse, 14

NC (*see* **Numerical control**)
Networks (*see also* Local area networks), 4, 130–34, 146
Neutral format, 135–38, 142
Note, 48, 54, 69, 70, 85
Numerical control, 4, 5, 96, 99, 107, 114, 152, 164
  distributed, 117

Offset, 26
Open Systems Interconnect (OSI), 133

Pack, 56
Pan (*see also* Scroll), 68
Patch, 76
Pathname, 29, 90
Pattern (*see also* Figure), 34, 152
Pick, 12, 14, 15, 22, 26, 27, 39, 41, 46, 47, 57
Pitfalls, 159
Plot, 20, 70, 159
Point, 35, 70, 84
Polling, 130
Polycode, 107
Postprocessor, 121, 122, 127

Printer, 19
Process planning, 107, 162, 164, 165
  computer-aided, 99, 103, 108–12, 149
  generative, 112
  variant, 111
Production, 4, 78, 96, 98, 102, 114, 165
Productivity, 79, 80, 107, 155, 160, 163
Programming, 1, 4, 5, 46, 78, 79, 99, 119–21, 126, 149, 152, 159, 162, 164, 165

Quality control, 8

Raster, 9, 11, 19, 20
Register, 119
Relocating algorithm, 15
Robot, 4, 8, 94
Root directory (*see also* Directory), 28, 29
Rotate, 57, 59, 68, 89
Rubber band, 36, 57

Scale, 57–59, 162
Screen:
  CRT, 8, 9, 11
  plasma, 9
  refresh, 8
  storage, 8, 9, 11
Scroll (*see also* Pan), 28
Security, 158
Selection criteria, 149, 150, 152, 154, 155, 164
Server, 129, 131, 134
Shading, 3, 11, 75, 76, 152, 164
Simulation, 92–94, 152
Software, 20, 149, 151, 159, 164, 165
Solids, 4, 74, 75, 152, 164
Sonic pen, 17

Spline, 42, 70, 71, 152
  Bezier, 42
  B-spline, 44
  Hermite, 42
Standards, 127, 134, 137, 143
  ANSI Y14.26M, 137, 138
  DIN 66025, 119
  IEEE 802, 132
  IGES, 138
  OSI, 133
  RS-232, 143
  RS-273, 119
  RS-449, 144
  VDAFS, 138
  V.24, 143
  X.21, 145
  X.25, 146
  X4.22, 12
Stream, 26
Stretch, 57
String, 41, 85, 122
Surface, 65, 69, 71–74, 87, 92, 152,
     162, 166
Symbol, 41

Tablet, 14
Tag, 46
Tangent, 37–39
Tape:
  magnetic, 5, 18, 129, 158
  paper, 117

Text, 41
Token passing, 130, 132, 165
Token ring (*see also* Standards), 132
Toolpath, 122–26, 163, 164
  pocket, 124
  profile, 124
  swarf, 126
Topology, 130, 131
Touch screen, 16
Trackball, 16
Translate, 57, 58, 89
Translator, 135, 136
Trap region, 27

Undelete, 56

Valuator, 12, 16, 27
Vector, 11, 20, 41, 57, 58
View, 68, 69
Voice, 17

Wildcard, 29
Window, 27, 28
Wireframe, 74, 75
Work layer (*see* Layer)
Workstation, 21, 164, 165

Zoom, 28, 68